THE OAKWOOD LIBRARY OF RAILWAY HISTORY

THE EAST FIFE CENTRAL RAILWAY
The Lochty Line

by
*Andrew Hajducki, Mike Jodeluk
and Alan Simpson*

THE OAKWOOD PRESS

© Oakwood Press & Andrew Hajducki, Mike Jodeluk & Alan Simpson 2015

British Library Cataloguing in Publication Data
A Record for this book is available from the British Library
ISBN 978 0 85361 738 9

Typeset by Oakwood Graphics.
Repro by PKmediaworks, Cranborne, Dorset.
Printed by Berforts Information Press Ltd, Stevenage, Herts.

All rights reserved. No part of this book may be reproduced or transmitted in any form or by any means, electronic or mechanical, including photocopying, recording or by any information storage and retrieval system, without permission from the Publisher in writing.

Lochty railtour, 20th January, 1962. *Norrie Forrest/Transport Treasury*

Front cover: 'J35' class 0-6-0 No. 64478 shunts at Montrave in the winter of 1960.
ColourRail

Rear cover, top: No. 9 on the Lochty Private Railway, 1970. *Mike Jodeluk*

Rear cover, bottom: Interested observers of the latter-day 'Fife Coast Express' at Knightsward in 1988. *Charles Naples*

Title page: Seal of the East Fife Central Railway. *S.M. Hajducki*

By the same authors and also published by the Oakwood Press, a trilogy of well-researched and highly readable books covering the railways that once served the beautiful East Neuk of Fife. Well illustrated, each book covers one of the three separate companies that were joined together to eventually form the fondly remembered coastal loop line of the North British Railway and its successors.

The St Andrews Railway (2008) ISBN 978 0 85361 673 3
The Anstruther and St Andrews Railway (2009) ISBN 978 0 85361 687 0
The Leven & East of Fife Railway (2013) ISBN 978 0 85361 728 0

Published by The Oakwood Press (Usk), P.O. Box 13, Usk, Mon., NP15 1YS.
E-mail: sales@oakwoodpress.co.uk
Website: www.oakwoodpress.co.uk

Contents

	Preface	5
Chapter One	Over the Hills and Far Away:	
	The Genesis of the East Fife Central 7	
Chapter Two	Rapid Progress:	
	The Building of the East Fife Central 19	
Chapter Three	Not as Expected:	
	The Early Years of the East Fife Central 27	
Chapter Four	Coal to the Rescue?:	
	The North British Era Continued 33	
Chapter Five	Through the Buffers:	
	The London & North Eastern Railway	43
Chapter Six	Infrequent Appearances:	
	The British Railways Era 47	
Chapter Seven	A Picturesque Piece of Country:	
	The East Fife Central Described 61	
Chapter Eight	Train Staffs and Traffic:	
	Working the Lochty Branch 71	
Chapter Nine	The Phoenix on the Farm:	
	The Lochty Private Railway 1967-1992 83	
Appendix One	A Brief Chronology of the Line 99	
Appendix Two	Traffic Figures 1900-1934 100	
	Sources, Acknowledgements and Bibliography	103
	Index	104

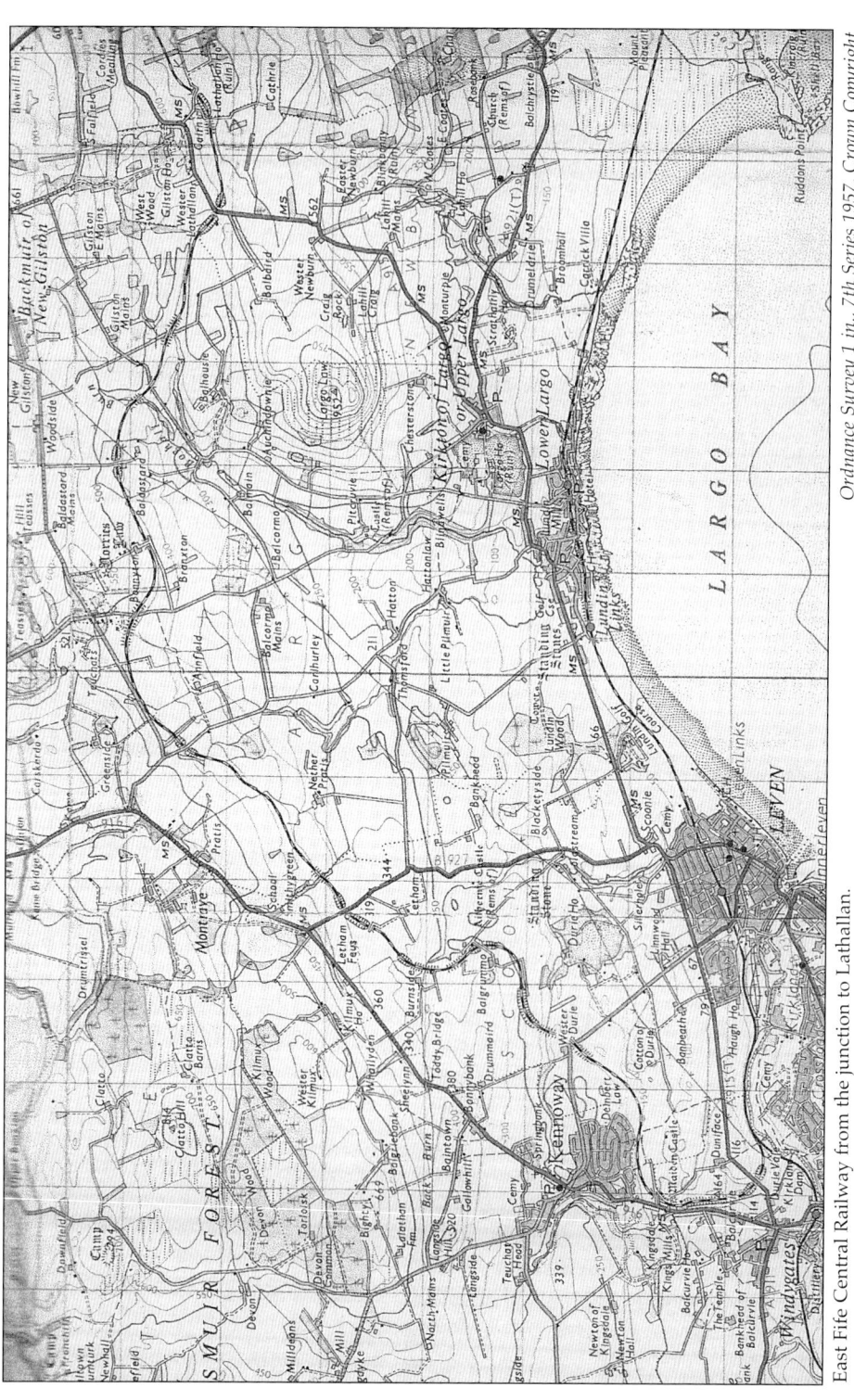

East Fife Central Railway from the junction to Lathallan.

Ordnance Survey 1 in., 7th Series 1957, Crown Copyright

Preface

The East Fife Central Railway, perhaps better known to all and sundry as the 'Lochty Line', was a rural byway with an interesting but somewhat sad history and, although it never lived up to the expectations of its promoters, it nevertheless managed to hang on to life until the era of Beeching and economic reality. From a junction with the Leven and East of Fife line near to the Haig distillery at Cameron Bridge, this most obscure of country railways valiantly climbed at a steady but taxing gradient through Kennoway and into that area of little known upland known as the Rigging of Fife. The line, having exhausted the meagre traffic possibilities of the village of Largoward and the farms around it then managed to end its 14½ mile wanderings by petering out near to the farm of Lochty, a place that was of little consequence and lay literally in the middle of nowhere. Such industrial potential as the line might have had was lost early on and for 50 years or more the lightly loaded thrice-weekly trains that served this unimportant limb of the North British managed to carry an ever-decreasing amount of coal and agricultural produce to the scattered communities of this beautiful inland area of the part of the county better known for its nearby seaside resorts and harbours of the East Neuk. A brief service of workmen's trains for the colliers of Largobeath carried the only regular passengers on the line and the branch had become well and truly forgotten long before its final demise in the summer of 1964. Then, in an unexpected coda, the last mile or so found a new life a couple of years later as the Lochty Private Railway where a totally out of place 'A4' express locomotive trundled up and down with a sole coach – a far cry from the days when it was the pride of the East Coast main line from Kings Cross to Edinburgh. Other stock followed but a quarter of a century later fate took another turn and what was Scotland's pioneer heritage railway line finally closed to all traffic in 1992 and from then on the rolling countryside of the Rigging once again resumed its quiet slumbers uninterrupted by the railway engine and clanking wagons of a previous era.

In this, the final volume of our railway rambles around the east of Fife, we take our leave and can only hope that, once the Galashiels line has re-opened, the Scottish Government will turn its pro-railway endeavours to two of the Fife lines that certainly deserve similar considerations, the branches to Leven and St Andrews. Alas, however, it is too late for the Lochty line to benefit from such largesse and to those who feel that this now forgotten lonely branch line should never have been closed there are undoubtedly more who think that, in retrospect, it should never have been built in the first place!

Edinburgh, Cellardyke, Stirling and Kirkcaldy,
St Andrews Day, 2014

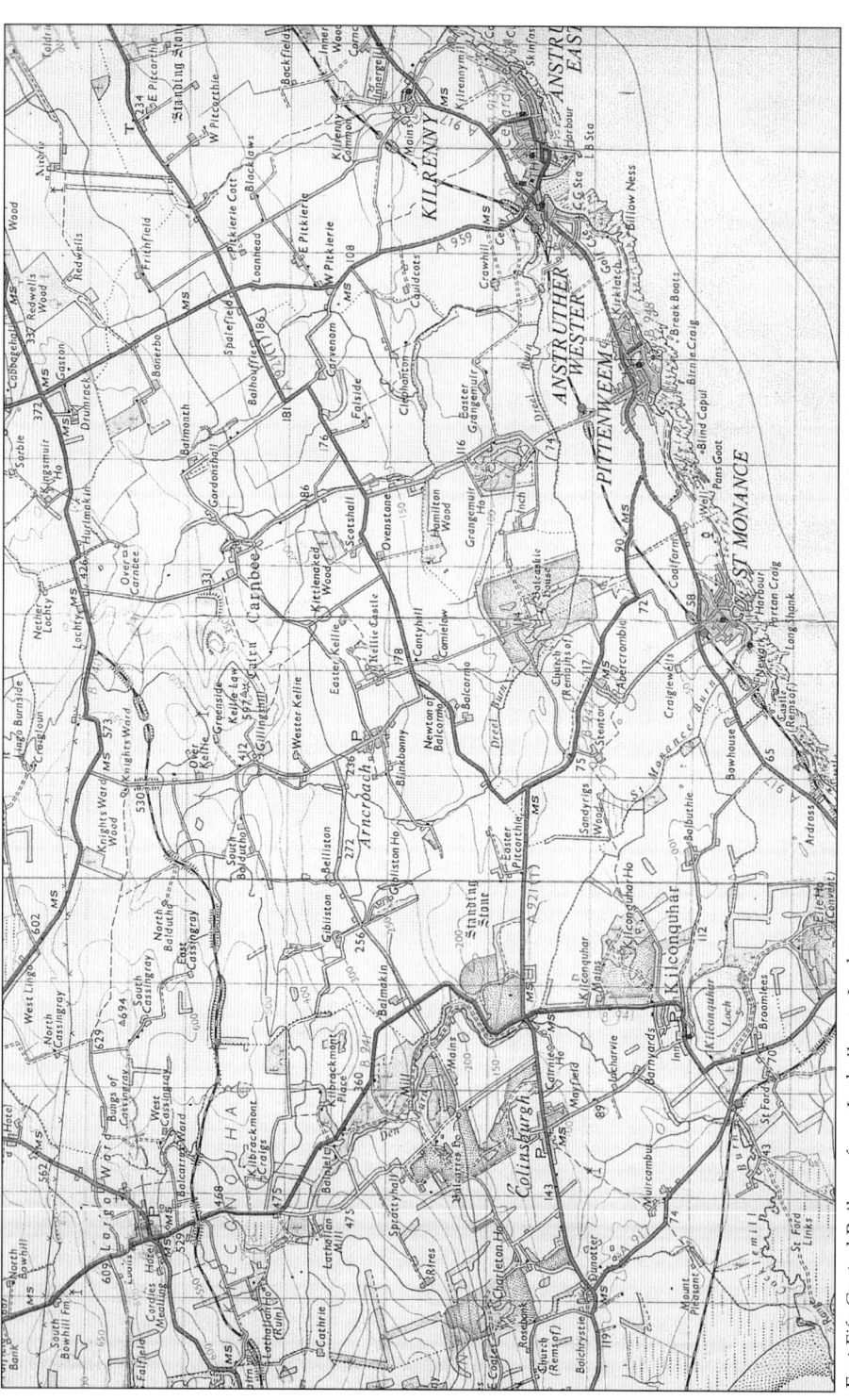

East Fife Central Railway from Lathallan to Lochty.

Ordnance Survey 1 in., 7th series 1957, Crown Copyright

Chapter One

Over the Hills and Far Away: The Genesis of the East Fife Central

'We can conceive nothing better calculated to improve the condition of the East Neuk than this railway.'
East of Fife Record, 4th November, 1892

Around the Rigging

With the completion of the railway line between Anstruther and St Andrews in 1887 the most easterly part of the Kingdom of Fife was now well served by the iron horse with the exception of one remaining area - the high ground lying to the north of the coastal plain of the East Neuk.* This area, where the railway had yet to invade, was known by the somewhat unusual but descriptive name of the 'Rigging of Fife', rigging being an old Scots word for a spine or backbone of an animal or ridge of a roof. The Rigging certainly lived up to its defining moniker and was a sandstone and igneous rampart which culminated in the volcanic intrusions of the Largo and Kellie Laws.† Behind these twin peaks lay an area of high undulating and often windswept pleasant hill pastures and open farmland interspersed with quiet woods and peaceful streams where by the end of the 19th century industry had barely shown its disfiguring hand. Relying largely on the fruits of their labours these highlands had an agricultural economy based upon the turnip, potato, barley, wheat, sheep and cattle and although an earlier account predicted that the steam engine in the form of the traction engine and threshing mill would soon be harbingers of change on the farms of the Rigging there were few signs that this revolution would come about within the lifetime of those Victorian Fifers.

Salubrious and pleasant

The population of the area was scattered in farms, prosperous landed estates and humble cottages and there were only two settlements of any size in the area which were to be served by the proposed East Fife Central Railway, namely Kennoway and Largoward. The former had a population of 805 according to the 1891 census and a contemporary account in the *Ordnance Gazetteer of Scotland* stated that Kennoway# 'occupies the southern slope of an eminence ... which commands a magnificent view of the waters of the Firth of Forth' and that although the village had dwindled with the decline in handloom weaving 'in the arrangements of its streets, and the style of some of its houses it retains indications of antiquity and it is prettier, cleaner and more substantial than the seaside villages or the collier villages of Fife while possessing a high reputation for salubrity'. Largoward,§ which had an 1891

---

* The East Neuk is the name given to the coastal part of Fife covering the parishes between Largo and Kingsbarns and terminating in the east at Fife Ness where the land then 'turns the corner' to face the storm-troubled North Sea.
† Largo Law only rises to a height of 965 ft above sea level and Kellie Law to merely half of that but both are conspicuous landmarks in an otherwise low-lying countryside.
# Kennoway, 'the place at the head' i.e. of the adjacent river gorge or den.
§ Largoward: 'an enclosed tract of land connected with the parish of Largo' on the coast although in fact Largoward was actually situated in the parish of Kilconquhar.

population of 1,018, was the undisputed agricultural centre of the Rigging and was described in the *Buildings of Scotland* as 'a rather shapeless but pleasant small village on a hillside'. One possible source of wealth (and perhaps bringing with it the concomitant poverty to the landscape) was under the ground for part of the Rigging lay on the eastern fringe of the East Fife coalfield which had already been exploited in the Leven and Wemyss area and, to a smaller and barely profitable extent, in certain small pits in the vicinity of Largoward where the coal measures extended over an area some three miles in length but, like all other local similar measures in the region, were said to include complicated and broken strata hemmed in on all sides by geological faults. Notwithstanding these qualifications there was a strong feeling that the mineral fields and coal seams could, and would, be profitably exploited to the benefit of all.

Opening moves

It was against this background of existing agricultural and expected mineral wealth amongst the hills that, on Wednesday 19th October, 1892, a meeting of gentlemen interested in the prospect of promoting a railway to serve the area was held within the offices of Edinburgh law agents Dundas & Wilson, CS.* The meeting was chaired by Major-General David Briggs of Strathairly House, Largo. At this meeting General Briggs, who was both a local landowner and a member of the recently formed Fife County Council, explained that he already had a plan of the proposed railway lines drawn up by an engineer, John Meik, and that in July of that year experimental borings had taken place on his land at Lochty† in the parish of Carnbee, and which lay a few miles to the north of Pittenweem and Anstruther. The coal at Lochty had been found at 10 fathoms (60 ft) - the sample being brought to the surface being of good quality and the seam being 3½ ft in width and of a considerable length. Mr Charles Carlow, the manager of the Fife Coal Co., had been duly impressed as had Dr Landale# and he therefore proposed that a line be constructed to take away the coal that was to be wrought and also to open up the district generally.

The railway scheme was an ambitious one with four lines totalling some 26 miles in all, running from a point between Leven and Cameron Bridge to Dairsie on the North British main line via Kennoway and Ceres, with a branch line to run across the central part of the area via Lochty to Stravithie on the Anstruther & St Andrews line. Apart from certain advantages which local travellers would gain - the distance from Leven to Dundee being shortened from 34 miles via Thornton to a mere 24, and from Leven to St Andrews from 28 miles to 20 - the new line would, in Major-General Briggs' words, be 'a benefit to the district ... [and] promote the interests of agriculture and mineral development'. Mr Meik told the meeting that the maximum gradient would be 1 in 70 and that there were no engineering difficulties of any importance and the meeting resolved to promote a Bill in the ensuing session of Parliament 'and guarantees to a considerable amount for this purpose were subscribed in the room, and it was expected that other gentlemen, who had not been able to attend, would contribute their quota'.

* 'Clerks to the Signet' - a prestigious legal title held (and still held) by this long established firm of Edinburgh law agents or solicitors.
† Lochty is an ancient name of uncertain and probably imported origin but probably means 'black or shining water' - it is strange that such an obscure place gave its name to a railway line!
# David Landale, LLD, a well-known mining engineer was partner in the firm of Landale, Frew & Gemmell, ME, of Glasgow.

Apart from Major-General Briggs these 'other gentlemen' included John Jordan, William Taylor, Edward Gorrell Baxter, and George Bradley Wieland. Jordan (1830-1914) was a Leith merchant having an office at 29 Constitution Street in that town - there is a memorial to him in South Leith Parish Church which states that 'he was an unfailing benefactor to this church and of many good causes in this town'. He was also coincidentally a Director of the North British Railway (NBR), the Fife Coal Co., the Commercial Bank of Scotland and, later on, the Wemyss Coal Co. Taylor, CA, of 168 West George Street, Glasgow, was the company accountant of William Baird & Co., a large industrial concern of ironfounders in the west as well as being described as 'a landed proprietor' as was Baxter who was said to be of Teasses, an estate lying to the south of Cupar. The most interesting of these was undoubtedly G.B. Wieland (1838-1905), described as being of 58, Marine Parade, Brighton. Born in England of parents who somewhat unusually were described as vaudeville artists, Wieland worked for the London & North Western Railway at Euston before moving north to become Secretary of the North British in 1874. An efficient and highly-regarded railway administrator, Wieland eventually became a Director of the NBR in March 1892 and from 1901 Chairman. Undoubtedly he was responsible for putting the finances of that company into order by driving down costs to the detriment of investment in rolling stock and locomotives - railway historian John Thomas perhaps unfairly said that 'when Wieland died, the fortunes of the NBR revived'. However, Wieland also had another side - he could be a ruthless and unforgiving opponent in the boardroom and perhaps could be said to have sailed close to the wind insofar as the spirit if not the law of the Companies Acts were concerned. An example of this was Wieland's purchase of the Letham estate close to Kennoway which Wieland believed would contain profitable seams of coal and borrowing the money from Taylor (and possibly given to him by Bairds) it was held in Taylor's name as mortgagee until conveyed directly to Wieland's son in 1895.

The contributions made towards meeting the initial survey and promotion costs came from a number of local landowners who were expecting to find the railway useful and monies advanced included £200 from Baxter and £100 each from Briggs, Thomas Buchan, Walter Irvine, the Earl of Crawford and Balcarres,* and the Trustees of the Lathallan estate.†

Well-placed optimism

There was a certain optimism about the future of the proposed line and in October 1892 the Surveyor-General of the Geological Survey of Scotland wrote to Briggs that,

> Speaking generally, I am of the opinion that the lines are well-planned with a view to developing the minerals – coals, limestone, etc – which occur in abundance in that part of the county. These isolated coal fields have been, and are to a great extent at the present time, locked up for want of railway communication.

The North British, while unwilling to subscribe any capital or even a contribution to the preliminary expenses, indicated that they would be willing to agree to the proposed junctions with their lines 'provided that these were constructed in a

---

* The Rt Hon. James Ludovic Lindsay, 26th Earl of Crawford was a noted astronomer and physicist whose estate was at Balcarres near Colinsburgh.
† The Lathallan estate, 'situated in Kilconquhar parish 2¼ miles NNW of Colinsburgh was owned by several generations of the Lumsdaine family and, from 1885, was held in trust for the more remote members of the family to whom it was bequeathed after the direct linear descendants of the last owners had died out.

manner satisfactory to their engineer' and further that they would be willing to work the line 'on suitable terms'. However, a glowing report appeared in the *Edinburgh Evening News* at the beginning of November and stated that,

> The promoters of the proposed East Fife Central Railway, which include some of the landowners on the route, are taking steps to introduce a bill in the opening session of Parliament. They are encouraged in this by the favour to which the scheme is received by the other proprietors interested in the district it is intended that the railway would open up. A number of landowners have agreed to give land to the promoters at its agricultural value and to take shares in the undertaking for the amount of purchase, while the necessary funds for the carrying of the bill through Parliament have been guaranteed … The railway is designed to open up the country between Leven and Teases [sic], Ceres and Dairsie, thereby forming a direct route from Leven to Dundee, by which a saving of ten miles will be effected. There is also a branch line to be taken off at a point near Teases and run in an easterly direction by Balhousie, Gilston and Lathallan. At a further point the line branches northwards, to form a junction with the Anstruther and St Andrews Railway near Stravithie station. The proposed railway will open up mineral fields which have been for many years closed because of the lack of such communication. On the estate at Letham several valuable seams of coal have been found and at Ceres there are some 17 seams of coal of an aggregate thickness of 60 feet, while at Teases very extensive fields of blue and white lime also exists. On the branch lines there are valuable seams of coal unworkable without a railway. At Lathallan Colliery alone the annual output is between 40,000 and 50,000 tons, all of which have to be carted away owing to a lack of railway facilities. Further east valuable seams of coal have been proved to exist on the estates of Lochty and Chesters.* A seam of upwards of 6 feet in thickness has been found at a depth of 18½ fathoms. In addition to mineral traffic the line will open up a new and important agricultural district…
>
> A report on the minerals is now being prepared by Dr Landale, ME - a man who is said to have a better knowledge of 'underground' Fife than many of the inhabitants of 'overground'. We have before us samples of the coal from the Chesters estates, and these are of a bright, hard, clean coal very superior, the mining engineers say, to that used to be sought from the same seams at Kellie.
>
> If the people welcome the project with enthusiasm, and give it a helping hand, success is certain, whereas if on the contrary they meet with apathy and indifference it may have to be relegated to an after generation. General Briggs, who has spent a great deal of time and labour in inaugurating the project has been successful in getting the head officials of the NBR to view the scheme very favourably, and it is expected that they will give every assistance in their power to see it carried through.

Dr Landale's perhaps optimistic report, entitled 'Memorandum as to Coal and other Minerals on the line of the proposed East Fife Central Railway', dated 26th October, 1892, referred to the coal measures already being worked in the vicinity of the proposed line at Largoward and Lathallan which were selling at a high price and where new seams could be mined and carried by the railway and the seams that could be opened up at Chesters and Lochty.

---

* Chesters was an estate lying a mile to the North of Lochty.

Four railways

The East Fife Central Railway Bill, which was published in January 1893, provided for an authorized share capital of £250,000 in £10 shares with borrowing powers of £83,333 (i.e. one-third of the authorized capital) and sought to have authorized the construction of four separate railways, namely:

Railway No. 1 – 12 miles, 2 furlongs, 8.30 chains in length, commencing in the parish of Scoonie by a junction with the Leven branch of the North British and terminating with the Edinburgh, Perth and Dundee section of the North British in the parish of Dairsie.
Railway No. 2 – 1 mile 3 furlongs, 5.70 chains in length, commencing by a junction with the Leven branch and terminating by a junction with the Railway No.1 both in the parish of Scoonie.
Railway No. 3 – 12 miles, 2 furlongs, 3.50 chains in length, commencing by a junction with Railway No. 1 in the parish of Ceres and terminating in the parish of Cameron, by a junction with the Anstruther & St Andrews Railway.
Railway No. 4 - 2 furlongs, 1.45 chains in the parish of Largo.

Railway No. 1 was, essentially, the main line and was to start 10 yards west of the centre of a bridge carrying the Leven to Cupar via Wester Durie road over the Leven branch (the former Leven & East of Fife line) a mile to to the north-west of the passenger station at Leven. Then it headed generally northwards via Braehead, Haughhouse, Cotton of Durie to Wester Durie, a mile south-east from Kennoway. The line then followed a winding course via Balgrummo, Burnside and Letham to Teuchats, where just south of the farm of that name a junction was to be made with Railway No. 3. From Teuchats the line proceeded northwards, skirting Teasses, and passing Fleesfauld (otherwise Fleecefaulds), Bandirran and Teassesmill before crossing the Craighall Burn and entering Ceres village. Turning north-eastwards the line then passed Newbigging of Ceres and followed the Ceres Burn through Pitscottie, Blebo and Kemback before crossing the River Eden and forming a junction with the North British main line at Dairsie Mains half a mile or so south-west of Dairsie station. For the first six miles or so the line would have climbed continuously at 1 in 70 and then would have descended on mainly the same gradient all the way to Dairsie.

Railway No. 2 would been a short line running from just east of Cameron Bridge station with a facing junction for trains travelling east, then to the north of the River Leven and west of both Kirkland and Duniface where it would then join Railway No. 1 at a trailing junction 500 yards west of Mireside and 400 yards north of Cotton of Durie. The line would have generally climbed the whole way at 1 in 70.

Railway No. 3 ran from the junction with Railway No.1 at Teuchats via Bonnyton and Baldastard to Lathallan Colliery, mainly on the level or on easy gradients of 1 in 100 or 1 in 200. From Lathallan the line travelled eastwards and passed to the south of Largoward, Cassingray and Baldutho, crossed the Arncroach to Knightsward road before swinging north-east to pass Lochty to where the summit of the line, at 550 feet above sea level, was reached at Nether Lochty. The line then began to descend through Chesters before turning north and passing East Carngour on a falling gradient of 1 in 70 before making a north-facing junction with the Anstruther & St Andrews line at Allanhill Bridge, 400 yards west of Stravithie station.

Railway No. 4 was a short connecting line whose purpose was to provide the third side of the triangle at Teuchats and to allow direct running between Stravithie and Dairsie via Railways Nos. 1 and 3.

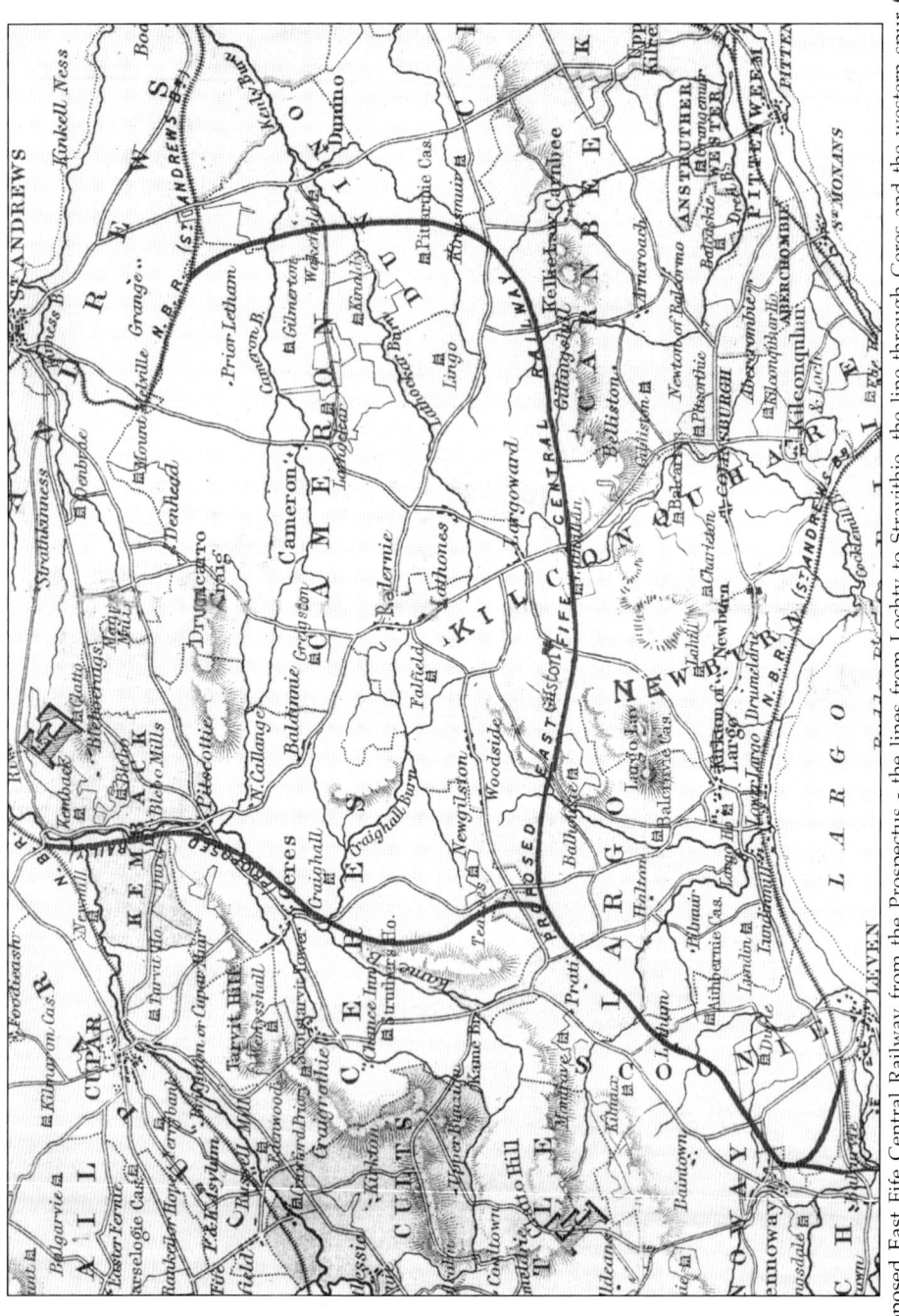

The proposed East Fife Central Railway from the Prospectus - the lines from Lochty to Stravithie, the line through Ceres and the western spur from Kennoway to Methil were never built.

Objections overcome

Although there were few objection from local landowners, and indeed the majority of those whose lands the East Fife Central was to pass through welcomed the scheme, especially if they were to be paid handsomely for the sale of their land, the principal objectors to the Bill were the North British Railway and the Caledonian Railway. The NBR contended that the new lines were unnecessary and that if constructed would practically duplicate their own route between Thornton and St Andrews via the main line and the East of Fife line and would abstract and divert traffic currently being carried by the North British. The proposed running powers over the Anstruther & St Andrews line between the junction of Railway No. 3 near to Stravithie and St Andrews were objected to as were the proposed junction works and it was said that the estimated expenditure would be insufficient for the works to be properly carried out. The Caledonian objections were that the new line would be worked by the North British which already had a monopoly of railway travel in Fife to the disadvantage of the Caley, that they wanted the same facilities on the new line as the NBR would enjoy and that by the opening of the Forth Bridge the NBR had not been carrying Caledonian traffic via Carstairs as they were obliged to do.

In the event negotiations at the behest of Wieland took place between the North British and the East of Fife Central, and on 28th April 1893 the two companies completed a working agreement (set out in the second schedule of the Act) whereby the East Fife Central would 'construct and complete as a first-class single line of railway with rails, chairs and sleepers for the permanent way of the weight and quality used and laid down in the manner observed in the North British Company's main line the proposed railways', together with all necessary stations, station masters' houses, gatekeepers' houses, goods sheds and sidings, signalling and 'speaking telegraph apparatus', all of which were to be constructed or provided in a good sufficient substantial and workmanlike manner to the reasonable satisfaction of the North British. In return the North British would work the line in perpetuity (or, after 10 years, upon the giving of six month's notice by the East Fife Central) and they were to maintain the line 'from and after the passing of the line by the Board of Trade'. The North British were to hire and dismiss the staff employed and were to collect the gross revenue and retain 50 per cent thereof, the balance being paid to the East of Fife Central company after the payment of certain expenses; a complicated arrangement was entered into whereby the North British in effect guaranteed a dividend of 4½ per cent to the paid-up shareholders of the East Fife Central. The running powers over the Anstruther & St Andrews were confirmed as was a provision whereby the Caledonian Railway could enjoy the same rights, powers and privileges as the North British in respect of the traffic passing over the line.

There was, accordingly, no further opposition and on 24th August, 1893 the East Fife Central Railway Act (56 & 57 Vict., cap. cxcvi) was passed. The authorized capital of the company was £250,000 in £10 shares and the first Directors were Wieland, Jordan, Taylor, Briggs and Baxter - as an observer noted 'From that time on, Wieland was in the driving seat and paid little heed to his fellow Directors'. However, it had already been realised that the East Fife Central scheme was over ambitious and accordingly unlikely to ever pay its way, depending as it would on unspecific coal traffic the majority of which was still speculative, very light passenger loadings and a moderate amount of agricultural and other traffic. Accordingly it was realised by Wieland and his fellow Directors that it might well prove impossible to raise the capital required and moreover that if the North British

Kennoway village, 1898.   *John Howard*

Largoward from the south, 1898.   *John Howard*

Lochty Farm, 1898.   *John Howard*

were to make up any dividends then they would only be prepared to do so if certain local landowners, colliery proprietors or others interested would put up financial guarantees that the traffic would be sufficient to allow them to do so. The scheme was again considered and a meeting was held on 10th November, 1893 in London between Wieland and John Conacher, General Manager of the NBR. Conacher noted that,

> Discussed this matter with Mr Wieland today on the basis of a line being constructed to Lathallan, and finally to Lochty, for mineral traffic but suitable for conversion at a small cost into a passenger line ... First step to be taken was to secure proper guarantees from the Land Owners or Mineral Lesees to work the Coal if the line was to be made.

Accordingly it was decided to cost out how much it would be to construct a line as far as Lochty. Estimates were, at the beginning of 1894, obtained from Messrs Thomas Meik & Sons, Edinburgh (the civil engineers acting for the Directors in succession to the late John Macrae) in respect of a single line exclusive of land from Leven/Cameron Bridge to Teasses Junction, Lathallan Road and Lochty Road, i.e. the first 14 miles or so of an amalgam of parts of Railways 1, 2 and 3 and it was found that the cost of a passenger line was estimated at £126,057 and £115,871 (dependent on the exact route) and of a goods line £99,602 and £89,820.

As far as Lochty

At the first statutory meeting of the new company, held on 14th February, 1894, Messrs Wieland, Jordan, Taylor, Baxter and Briggs were all present, as was the company Secretary, solicitor Ralph Dundas of Dundas & Wilson. Wieland was in the chair and the Directors all agreed to apply for 20 shares each so as to qualify them for office. Thereafter guarantees and undertakings were laid on the table by Wieland, Jordan, Baxter and Briggs as individuals undertaking to make up any deficiencies for a period of five years in the event of the gross annual traffic from the 14½ miles of railway now being proposed to be constructed not being sufficient to pay 3 per cent upon a sum proposed to be advanced by the NBR for the construction of the said 14½ miles and the same was signed by these gentlemen. Major-General Briggs undertook to do what he could to get similar guarantees from other persons resident in the district (including, in April 1894, a guarantee from the Earl of Crawford which was limited to a maximum of £400 in any one year), while the question of whether or not a siding should be constructed to serve Mr Baxter's Teasses Limeworks was left entirely in the Chairman's hands.

On 13th March Wieland wrote to Conacher, enclosing the guarantees and estimates and asked him to consider which of the estimates was most suitable, together with a draft agreement. Further correspondence enquired as to why the East Fife Central Directors now wished the line to connect with the North British close to Cameron Bridge and it was said that this alteration would provide better access to Leven and Methil Docks and a proposal was made that the East Fife Central Railway be wound up and its powers be transferred to the North British, subject to sufficient guarantees being given. On 14th May the East Fife Central Board met again and Wieland explained that he had had various meetings with Conacher in relation to the North British advancing the construction costs of the line to Lochty but that the new route was outside the limits of deviation of route permitted under the 1893 Act and that a new Act would be required if Parliamentary permission to the line now proposed was to be given. The Directors unanimously agreed that they would not, however, abandon their undertaking. At a subsequent Board meeting, held on 18th July, they agreed to make a joint application with the North British for Parliamentary powers and that although they could not concede to the North British extending the guarantees to cover a period of seven years (they already having had a hard enough task in securing five-year guarantees) they would undertake 'upon the completion of said mineral railway to make application to Parliament either alone or in conjunction with the North British Company for a transfer of the powers of their company* to the North British' and that in the event to the North British agreeing to the same, of concluding a formal agreement with them. Then on 13th September the North British minutes report the terms of the agreement entered into with the East Fife Central, which were essentially as above with a few minor amendments, and the Board ratified the same.

The Minute of Agreement was signed on 30th October and on 6th November, 1894 a Bill of Quantities was submitted and signed by the contractor, John Howard of London† who tendered to construct the line for £84,457 with a deduction of £8,531 14s. 0d. if 70 lb. instead of 'NB pattern 84lbs' rails were used. The estimated cost of the land to be acquired was £15,000. The tender was accepted, subject to some modifications including a reduction of £7,000 after objections to the cost.

The line to be built

Thus what had started out as a complex interlocking series of lines covering the whole of the area ended up in a single 14 mile branch line which was now to leave the Leven line at East of Fife Central Junction, a west-facing junction situated half a mile to the east of Cameron Bridge station. It would then run northwards for a short distance parallel to the Leven to St Andrews road on the route of Railway No. 2 before joining Railway No.1 near Cotton of Durie and continue on its route south of Kennoway to Wester Durie and on to Teuchats where Railway No. 3 was then followed via Lathallan to Lochty where the line abruptly terminated in splendid isolation in field lying to the south of the Crail to Cupar road a couple of hundred yards short of the farm of that name. There were goods stations and public sidings at Kennoway (1 mile 67 chains from East Fife Central Junction), a short distance from the village of that name and Montrave (6 miles 4 chains from the junction), a somewhat isolated spot fairly near to and taking the name of the Montrave estate#

* The official name of the Lochty branch as 'East Fife Central Railway' (EFCR) was only finally decided upon by John Conacher in June 1896.
† This firm, whose registered office was at 17 Victoria Street, London, SW, had already been engaged on the Kirkcaldy & District Railway and Seafield Dock scheme in Fife and went on subsequently to construct the Aberlady, Gullane and North Berwick Railway - for the latter see A. Hajducki, *The North Berwick and Gullane Branch Lines,* Oakwood Press,1992. Wieland and Howard were business associates, prior to and after the EFCR contract, and possibly the contract should never have been entered into without further scrutiny.
# Montrave is a Pictish name appropriately meaning 'the good (or extensive) farm' but the station was originally to have been known as Greenside after the farm of that name lying much closer to the north of the line but was renamed in February 1897 to avoid confusion with Greenside on the North Eastern Railway in England and the already existing Greenside Junction on the North British.

of Sir John Gilmour. Gilmour (1845-1920) was a prominent Conservative and Scottish Unionist politician who was created the First Baronet of Lundin and Montrave in 1897 and came from family of Renfrewshire shipowners and businessmen who purchased the Montrave estate in 1873. He became a notable farmer and formed the Montrave stud as well as being a respected breeder of Clydesdale horses, shorthorn cattle and pedigree sheep, causing him to become a frequent livestock customer of Montrave station.* The next station to the east was Largoward, lying close to the small settlement of that name at the crossroads of Kilconquhar to Peat Inn and Largo to St Andrews roads. Further on lay Lochty, the terminus surrounded by green fields but enjoying a panoramic view to perhaps make up for its absence of almost anything else. After the line was built there were added a number of private sidings built to serve farms and collieries en route but a belated but half-hearted attempt to continue the line from Teuchats to Cupar was abandoned in January 1895 since there was no way in which even the optimistic promoters could see how the additional line would pay its way.

There were, however, still some doubts as to whether the construction of even that part of the line as far as Lochty could be justified on economic grounds alone and in May 1895 it was reported that workmen were still engaged on drilling for coal in the vicinity of Lochty Farm and that 'so far the work has not turned out to be so successful as was anticipated and the making of the new railway has been stopped in the meantime or until it can be fully ascertained whether sufficient coal is lying under the surface so as to justify the opening of a colliery'. Notwithstanding this unfortunate turn of events and even before any construction work could practically be undertaken, Parliamentary approval had to be obtained and on 16th July, 1895 the North British Railway Act 1895 (58 & 59 Vict., cap. cli) was passed. This provided for a series of deviations to reflect the route of the Lochty branch as eventually built and in Section 21 stated that the Board of Trade could, at any time, order that any lines built could be converted into passenger lines. Section 39 provided that on the expiry of 12 months from the passing of the Act or on satisfactory completion of the line to Lochty, whichever happened first, the East Fife Central company 'shall be dissolved except for the purpose of winding up their affairs and the undertaking of that company shall as from that date be amalgamated with the undertaking of the [North British] company'. With the benefit of hindsight it is perhaps fortunate that the line from Lochty to Stravithie was never constructed and it is hard to see what traffic it could have reasonably enjoyed given the uncertainty of there being any real reserves of coal in the area and the fact that had the line been made to rely on agricultural traffic. The absence of any settlements east of Largo would not have presaged a profitable future and that the comparative financial failure of the Anstruther and St Andrews Railway would have hardly encouraged the building of a link at Stravithie.

---

* His son, the second baronet, also Sir John Gilmour, was the MP for Glasgow Pollok, the Secretary of State for Scotland in 1924-26, Minister of Agriculture in 1931 and Home Secretary between 1932 and 1935. His grandson, the third baronet, was Sir John Edward Gilmour (1912-2007), MP for East Fife and a prominent campaigner in the fight to save the St Andrews to Leven Railway in the 1960s. The family seat, Montrave House, was largely demolished in 1970 but the estate is still owned by the family.

East Fife Central Junction looking west to Cameron Bridge prior to opening showing the signals not yet brought into use and the Leven & East of Fife line before it was doubled between Thornton and Leven in 1910.
John Howard

John Howard's steam navvy in use at Letham.
John Howard

Chapter Two

Rapid Progress:
The Building of the East Fife Central

'A pug engine has arrived this week and is only awaiting the
laying of the service rails ...'
East of Fife Record, 10th January, 1896

Construction commences

On 9th August, 1895 the East Fife Central Directors resolved to proceed with the immediate construction of their railway on obtaining financial guarantees from the Lathallan Trustees or beneficiaries, Douglas Irvine and Sir Alexander Moncrieff, to bear a share of any loss in the event of the gross traffic not yielding 3 per cent on the sum expended. It was explained that the agreement as regards Lathallan had been signed by two of the beneficiaries and that the only beneficiary who had not signed was a married lady whose husband was in Australia and it was resolved to take her signature 'in the hope that her husband would confirm it'. Guarantees were eventually forthcoming from Sir Alexander Moncrieff (4th September, 1895, 'a maximum of £100 in any year and not exceeding 1/30th of any shortfall') and, in place of that from Douglas Irvine, a proprietor who was unable to give a guarantee until he had let all of his coal, Major-General Briggs gave a further guarantee not to exceed £100 in any one year although he wanted to insist, rather perversely, that the construction of the line should commence simultaneously at both ends.

In October 1895 the contract between Howard and the East Fife Central was finally settled in the sum of £56,474 5s. 7d. exclusive of the cost of the permanent way and notices were served on the landowners over which the first four miles of line from Cameron Bridge were to run that their lands were now required for construction purposes. By the following month all the landowners had agreed to the arrangements proposed and Howard had moved the last of his plant and equipment to a field near Myreside farm near Kennoway, where the *East Fife Record* of 15th November reported that 'workmen are putting up fencing where it is understood that some sheds etc. are now being erected'. East Fife Central Junction was now under construction and on 4th December, 1895 Major Marindin of the Board of Trade sanctioned the use of the temporary junction 'now under construction, with the North British single line branch between Cameron Bridge and Leven stations'. The points were worked from a ground frame locked by a tablet for the section of line. Work was, however, already under way and on 22nd November the *East of Fife Record* had reported that,

> The contractor, Mr Howard, has now got squads of men employed at various points along the route of the new line. The course has been staked out, and fencers are engaged lining off the road. At the point where the line joins the main railway squads are busy cutting the track, but so far the number of navvies is not large, the cuttings not being very heavy. The store houses and offices are in the course of erection near Kennoway, a staff of joiners promising to have them complete within a few days. Quarrying operations at the Spate have been suspended owing to the inflow of water, but a powerful pumping engine is being fitted up to cope with this drawback. There appears to be no lack of labourers, although it will be about New Year before these are required in large numbers. The majority of these presently resort to Leven, but like the foreman etc. they will eventually find it necessary to seek houses nearer the work.

The pugs arrive

Shortly before Christmas it was reported that upwards of 200 workmen were employed that week on the construction works and on 10th January the same paper informed its readers that,

> The work is making rapid progress. The bridge on the high road at Wester Durie Farm is quickly approaching completion, and this week also altering the course of the burn in Durie Vale field - opposite which some of the workmen are at present busily engaged on a deep cutting - has been effected. A 'pug' engine has arrived this week, and is only awaiting the laying of the 'service' rails to be of much service to the contractors.

The 'pug' engine was one of three 0-4-0 outside-cylinder saddle-tanks used on the contract and which rejoiced in the names of *Mabel, Alice* and *Rose*. The first of these, *Mabel*, an Andrew Barclay locomotive (No. 755 of 1895 with 12 in. x 20 in. cylinders) was purchased new for the project, while *Alice* had previously been at work on a previous Fife contract of Howard namely the Kirkcaldy & District Railway where she had borne the name *Stockton*. *Rose* was of unknown origin and was a Barclay outside-cylinder box-tank locomotive which had born the rather pedestrian name of *HB*.

A major innovation on the contract, at least insofar as the inhabitants of the area who had not seen such a formidable beast before, was the use of 'steam navvy', a fearsome steam-powered machine with a large bucket and grab that had originated in America in the 1870s. These had seen comparatively little use in Britain until now although they had been used on major contracts such as the Manchester Ship Canal, the Great Central Railway London extension and the North British Railway's West Highland line. On 15th January, 1896 the Directors were informed that although not all of the land purchases had gone quite as smoothly as they might have hoped, 5,000 cubic yards of soil had already been excavated from the cuttings and used in other earthworks and that generally good progress had been made, despite the weather.

By the end of February materials for one mile of permanent way was being requested to be delivered to the junction and the first sum, amounting to £2,307, had been paid to the contractor. On 17th April the *Record* noted that,

> Rapid progress continues to mark the construction of this line, the steam navvy now being cast at another mound, while a large number of horses are engaged at the waggons. The class of workman appears to be steadier. An extra policeman has been stationed in the Kennoway district chiefly to supervise the new works, the main body of men being now engaged outside the immediate neighbourhood of Kennoway.

Pushing forward

The *East of Fife Record* of 22nd May reported that,

> Favoured with weather such as has been seldom experienced for steadiness and dryness, the operations in connection with the new railway have been pushed forward under propitious circumstances. Some four hundred men are engaged at the work, under the superintendence of Mr Alex. Clark, Mr Howard's general manager, and Mr John Scott, the local manager. Day and night shifts have been on duty for the past three weeks at the bridges and approaches to the west of Leven road; night squads will also

be engaged below Balgrummo farm. One of the heaviest cuttings yet tackled is to be faced here, and when this is finished access will be obtained to the junction, a question of eight or ten days, and enable the men to carry the rails on to the Burnside. A bridge at the old right-of-way to Birell's farm is to be finished shortly. Some three and a half miles of the road are now cut, and for a mile and a half of this the permanent way is laid ... It is pleased to note that the men have settled down to their quarters, a better class of navvies have gathered, and now the greatest orderliness marks their conduct. This is appreciated by the residenters, and in return the men find themselves received with a cordiality which for so long as the rougher element asserted itself they could not expect. In the matter of lodgings, the inhabitants are found very accommodating and altogether the relations existing between them and are such as must be pleasing to the strangers. The work has so far being pushed on without a serious accident, a tribute to the care exercised by the manager and his foremen. Mr Scott, like Mr Clark, has a long experience of this class of work, something like thirty-three years having been spent at it, his duties taking him over the whole of the United Kingdom. The bulk of the material for the new line has been detrained at Leven and Cameron Bridge ... [but] as the line is carried east more demand will be made upon the Lundin Links and Largo stations.

Little was subsequently heard of any of the proposed but unbuilt sections of the East Fife Central and in January 1897 the *Record* commented that although there was once a plan for a line from Leven to Dairsie 'so far as the public are concerned, there has been something of the 'dark horse' about this scheme all along'. This had been confirmed by an advertisement for sale of a country baking business in the *Scotsman* of 15th April, 1896 which included the statement that, 'The Fife Central Railway, which is now in progress, is expected to give a great impetus to the trade of Ceres and district'.

On 16th October, 1896 the EFCR was given a petition signed by some 125 'tenant farmers, householders and others' asking for the erection of a station at West Gilston Mains between Baldastard and Largoward. But the Lochty branch moved forward and on 28th May, 1897 it was said that in Largoward,

> Seven miles of permanent rails have now been laid on the new railway, and the strangers engaged have left the village, while local workmen are conveyed to and from work in waggons drawn by a pug, which wags have dubbed 'The Flying Scotchman'. The exodus of the navvies has lessened the stir, though nothing exceptionally wrong can be laid to their charge.

A fortnight later it was reported that the section working eastwards had now reached Baldastard and temporary rails had been laid as far as this point while the section working westwards from Lochty was 'pushing on rapidly' and that 'a junction of the two squads is within measurable distance'. By now most of the compensation claims for neighbouring landowners had been dealt with and when Sir John Gilmour requested that a culvert be made under the line so as to allow the passage of his foxhounds it was recommended that the full cost of this be met 'for reasons of sentiment'. On 30th July the *Record* stated that,

> The operations in connection with the ... railway have begun at the back of Kellie Law, and in the watershed which supplies Anstruther and Pittenweem with water, a cutting of from 20 to 25 feet deep, has been made through the crest of rock which extends northwards from Kellie Law. In cutting through this whinstone rock, two springs of water have been met with, and if the rock was fairly cut through they will likely land into softer and wet material. The fall of the railway is eastwards all the way to Over

The contractor's pug engine *Rose* at the Cairn bridge near Lathallan.   *John Howard*

Pug engine *Alice* hauling a train of tipper wagons at Teuchats Road bridge.   *John Howard*

Kellie, and all the water so collected will naturally fall into the watershed, which supplies Anstruther and Pittenweem with water. There is no doubt that through their operations there will be a considerable increase in the dry weather flow of the Anstruther and Pittenweem burn.

Obstacles removed

By February of 1898 the only remaining major obstacle was the cutting between Knightsward and Lochty through an outcrop of hard volcanic rock. The cutting was described by the contractor as being 'the deepest on the line and the worst on account of the rock which has been encountered'. In the following month 90 per cent of the bridges and culverts were completed, 80 per cent of the permanent way had been laid and about 60 per cent ballasted while most of the work on the four stations had been completed. Work continued, notwithstanding concern being expressed over the insanitary condition of the navvy huts at Lochty and in March the Knightsward cutting was complete and a number of the workmen paid off. The *Record* of 18th March reported that,

> The railway will soon be ready for traffic. The connection between the present eastern terminus of the line and the East of Fife Railway [i.e. the Anstruther & St Andrews Railway] at Allanhill Bridge, two miles south of St Andrews, and for which Parliamentary powers have been obtained, has been postponed for the present. A new freestone quarry on Stravithie Moor has lately been opened and should it turn out as expected, it will be a valuable feeder to the new line which passes close by.

The bridge referred to at Allanhill, which still exists and is under a minor public road leading to Gilmerton House and the freestone quarry had been provided with a private siding leading off the Anstruther & St Andrews line.

In July it was said that the final cutting was completed and that a ballast train now entered the station on a daily basis. The navvies' wooden huts had all been removed in the previous month since workmen were now conveyed to the terminus by train and that since this was done, it was said that all was now quiet in the area 'especially on pay Saturdays, on which many lively scenes were witnessed during the past winter'.

It would now appear that the line was ready for traffic and a private outing by rail took place as according to the *Leven Advertiser* of 4th August,

Kennoway station complete, 1898. *John Howard*

Montrave station with *Mabel* approaching from the east, 1898. *John Howard*

The impressive Largo Road bridge at Montrave. Here the gradients changed from 1 in 70 to a short level section. *John Howard*

Largoward station under construction with the still surviving goods office on the right.
John Howard

The pretty lines of *Mabel* shown to good effect at Baldutho bridge near Montrave. *John Howard*

Lochty station looking east shortly before opening in 1898.   *John Howard*

To a company of seven gentlemen hailing from Kennoway, Friday last [i.e. 29th July] will undoubtedly rank as a red-letter day on account of a pleasant and unique excursion which they were that day privileged to enjoy. The East Fife Central Railway has just been completed as far as Lochty, which in the meantime is the terminus, and a few friends who are on holiday in their native place, along with some residents, were anxious to get a run up the new line. The realisation of wishes, however, seemed quite beyond reach, until it was proposed that a deputation should wait on one of the leading officials of the railway and lay the matter before him. This gentleman, in a most obliging manner, at once agreed to the idea, and promised to do what he could in order that they might have their first trip by rail from Kennoway station. The result was that, including the host, eight good men and true started in a train from the bottom of the brae about nine o'clock on Friday morning. The train consisted of the engine and two goods waggons, and seats were supplied by forms placed on either side of a waggon. This style of railway travelling was certainly a long way removed from the ease and luxury associated with the first-class carriages of the present day, but it had its charms. During their progress along the route, the several places passed were duly noted, and their appearance from this new point of view occasionally gave rise to witty remarks on the part of some members of the company. In this way the journey to Lochty was completed, when, on the invitation of their host, an adjournment was made to a room in the station buildings, in which a light lunch was done ample justice to, and, is customary at all such functions, a little speech-making was afterwards indulged in.

After lunch the party travelled on to St Andrews by road and onwards by rail back to Leven via Anstruther before returning to Kennoway and a champagne supper at the Swan hotel.*

Much of the contractor's equipment remained on site until on 14th and 15th March, 1899 it was put up for sale by auction at Kennoway but by that time *Mabel* and *Alice* had been sold, the former to James Young & Co. who then used it on the construction of the Caledonian line from Cathcart to Newton in the Glasgow suburbs before being sold on to William Baird & Co. Ltd for use at the Lugar Ironworks near Cumnock and later working at Auchincruive Colliery at Annbank. *Rose* remained with Howard and was subsequently used by them on the construction of the Aberlady and Gullane line which was opened to traffic in April 1898.

* The Swan Hotel in New Road, Kennoway is still open for business more than a century later although champagne suppers are, one suspects, of a rarer occasion at the present time!

Chapter Three

Not as Expected:
The Early Years of the East Fife Central

'Traffic on this branch has not increased as we would have wished.'
Report to the NBR District Traffic Superintendent, 23rd June, 1900

Open for traffic

The *Leven Advertiser* of 11th August, 1898 reported that on Friday 4th August the East Fife Central line had been formally opened by the contractors handing the works over to the North British in the presence of a number of railway dignitaries including its Chief Superintendent, Chief Engineer, the Superintendent of the NBR Northern Section, the Chief Inspector of Lines 'Mr Arnott of Burntisland, Mr Clark CE, Mr Nominco etc.' In taking over the line the Chief Superintendent, David Deuchars, apparently expressed himself as being satisfied with the works 'and it was said that 'several parties have been over the line recently and have all expressed themselves perfectly satisfied with its construction'. A few days later, on 16th August, 1898, the North British issued the following circular signed by John Conacher, as General Manager.

> The staff are hereby informed that the East of Fife Central line, which connects with the Leven branch between Cameron Bridge and Leven stations, will be opened for goods and mineral traffic on Sunday 21st August, 1898. The names of the stations on the new line are Kennoway, Montrave, Largoward and Lochty.*

There was only one further hurdle to clear, that of the official inspection by the Board of Trade of the junction and signal box at East of Fife Central Junction since although the Lochty line was classified, at least in the meantime, as a mineral-only line it joined the passenger-carrying Leven and East of Fife line here and accordingly the junction with that line required to be officially inspected. This was done on Wednesday 24th August when Major Sir Francis Marindin, the Board of Trade inspector, approved of the new arrangements, subject to some trees being cut back to improve the view of the up starting signal and the installation of timber guards alongside the new loop at the junction where it was bisected by an occupation crossing.

However, the opening of the new railway preceded the inspection of the junction as, according to the *East of Fife Record* of 26th August, the line was opened as advertised at mid-day on Sunday 21st August† and under the heading of 'Carnbee' the paper reported that,

> The parishioners in the northern part of the parish were much surprised to observe a train steam into Lochty station, the terminus of the railway, on Sunday forenoon, accompanied by a number of the official staff of the N.B. Railway, who seemed to make a thorough inspection of the various points, sidings, &c. about the station. After a stay

---

* The NBR always referred to the line by its full name and never as the Lochty Branch but the 1914 General Appendix did refer to it as the 'Montrave Branch' (BR/RB(S)/3/28).
† There appears to be some confusion as to this date because the first *public* service would surely have been on Monday 22nd August there being at that time no normal Sunday service on either the Lochty line or the connecting East Fife line at Leven.

27

of about two hours the train and attendants again left for the west. It seems that the terminus which was opened for the arrival and despatch of goods and mineral traffic on Monday this week, had to undergo the usual inspection on such occasions by the staff, for which Sunday owing to the suspension of traffic on the Leven section with which the Fife Central forms a connection was found to be the most suitable day.

While elsewhere in the same edition it was said that 'the district through which the line runs is rich in minerals, and it should prove a paying concern to the North British, then it will be extended to Stravithie, and passenger trains run thereon' while its rival, the *Leven Advertiser* had already pointed out in its report of August 11th,

The line was originally intended for mineral traffic only, but as the district which it traverses is not only richly mineral but is also populated, there is no reason why the North British Railway company should not make it a more popular route by adding a passenger service.

The *Advertiser* however contained this most illuminating report in its issue of Thursday 25th August,

EAST FIFE CENTRAL RAILWAY

Sunday was a most important day in the history of this line, as it was on that day that the first officially billed train left Leven station to go over the route. A six wheeled engine, two carriages and a brake van started from Leven station at 10 a.m. with a considerable number of officials and the general public, all anxious to view the fine strath opened up by the new line. On approaching the Central Junction, midway between Leven and Cameron Bridge, all was found to be in readiness.

One of the outstanding reasons for the selection of the 21st for the opening day was because of the great amount of work in the way of telegraph connections joining up signalling apparatus etc., work that could not readily have been undertaken on a week day without causing serious delays to the main line traffic. A large staff of workmen had been engaged on this since daylight.

Kennoway was the first station. Here Mr. Oliphant acts as stationmaster.* As at the other stations along the route, provision is made for the construction of passenger platforms† but in the meantime only loading embankments are built along with the sidings.

A run through the beautiful policies of Durie brought them to Greenside (i.e. Montrave). No permanent appointment of a stationmaster has been made here but at Largoward Mr Clyne is in charge. The line skirts the village, and is within easy reach of the new pit, the shaft of which has been sunk for Messrs Street, Dunfermline.# A most extensive and beautiful view of Fife is obtained from this elevation but at Lochty, where the train is now 440 ft above the elevation of the Junction, the prospect is even finer and wider. Kellie Law blocked the line of view to the south-west but the sweep of the coast from St Monans right across the East Neuk, all like a lovely landscape garden, could be seen. Mr W. Nicoll acts as stationmaster here.

Those with a knowledge of the countryside could indicate along the road points where rich mineral fields lay waiting to be developed and the company was convinced the railway has yet an important future in store for it. A couple of hours was allowed at Lochty for those who desired to inspect the terminus of the district. Pittenweem is distant some 3½ miles. One stop was made on the run back to Leven and, allowing for this, the 15½ miles was accomplished in thirty-two minutes.

The mode of working is to be by train staff but, as in the meantime no passenger trains will be run over the line, no fixed signals or interlocking has been put in.

* The North British in fact used the term 'station agent' rather than 'station master'.
† These, of course, were not constructed until in 1913 the Largobeath Colliery workmen's trains were run (*see Chapter Four*).
\# This is a reference to Messrs Street Bros of the Appin Fireclay Works of Dunfermline.

Not as expected

There was, however, no public advertisement of the opening and when the chief goods manager of the North British wrote to Conacher suggesting that such be made, it was decided not to as the opening would 'doubtless be noticed by the local populance'. In October 1898 a letter was received by the North British from a local landowner, Major Sprot of Stravithie House at Dunino, asking if and when the proposed extension from Lochty to Stravithie would be undertaken.* Conacher replied that that part of the undertaking had been abandoned 'on the failure of the East Fife Central Railway to carry out any part of their schemes'. At the same time it was noted that 'until we have had experience of the working of the portion of the line we have already constructed, it was premature to undertake any further liability'. In March 1899 a letter was received by the Board of Trade in London from the County Clerk of Fife complaining that the Lochty line had been certified by their inspector as having been fit for passengers, goods, coal and cattle traffic and that they should forthwith open it to passenger traffic. The North British, to whom the matter was referred, replied that the line had in fact no passenger stations on it and that it had not been approved of for passenger traffic by the Board of Trade and that they did not intend to open the line to passengers in the meantime.

Initial traffic on the line was disappointing and the returns for the first complete year of service to 31st August, 1899 in respect of local traffic between East Fife Central stations amounted to £19 2s. 7d. for goods and 9s. 8d. for minerals, for traffic between East Fife Central and North British stations £579 18s. 1d. for goods, £377 0s. 10d. for minerals and £10 5s. 4d. for livestock while the equivalent figures for traffic between East Fife Central and stations beyond the North British amounted to £103 2s. 7d., £33 17s. 2d. and 8s. 5d. respectively. The majority of the traffic was agricultural in nature and at least in the early years coal traffic was negligible, the colliery at Lathallan being closed in November 1899,† the two remaining collieries at Baldastard and Largoward providing little traffic and the extensive trial bores and search for coal in the Lochty area coming to nothing.

On 22nd August, 1900 the Lathallan estate was sold by public roup (auction) and advertised as follows,

> There are eight different seams of coal worked by the estate - one of them Lathallan Splint coal seam, reported by mining engineers as the best coal in Fife, commanding a landsale with a demand greater than supply. The last colliery working of importance ended in 1896, but boreholes put down since then have found seams at greater levels. Since the colliery opened the East Fife Central Railway has been constructed through the lands connecting the coalfield (previously worked by land sale only) with railway works and the shipping ports of Methil and Burntisland. Largo Ward station (meantime for goods and minerals only, is on the estate.

With the failure of the mineral traffic to take off as expected the management of the North British was beginning to become aware that the Lochty line was not such

---

* Alexander Sprot (1853-1929) was a soldier with a distinguished career who took an interest in local affairs, and in particular in railway matters; later knighted, his chief contribution to history is possibly that, as a Conservative, he defeated the Liberal Prime Minister H.H.Asquith as MP for East Fife in 1918. Himself defeated in 1924 he then became MP for North Lanarkshire until replaced by the young Jenny Lee, the Fife-born Socialist politician who later married Aneurin Bevan.

† Situated west of Largoward, between the A915 road and Lathallan House, this colliery was never directly rail served but is thought to have provided some traffic at Largoward in the first year of the railway's operation.

a sound investment as it had first seemed. In June 1900 a letter was sent to the chief goods manager in Glasgow from one of his subordinates, John Stewart, pointing out that the traffic was not improving on the line and, by way of illustration, on the sixth of that month the daily goods train had left Leven with four loaded wagons and four empties. It left one loaded wagon at Kennoway and the rest at Montrave and on the return journey lifted four wagons of minerals from Largoward and one goods and one mineral wagon at Montrave. On the following day the train had one mineral, one goods and four empties leaving Leven, one loaded and three empties were left at Montrave and two loads left at Kennoway. 'I think that it should be seriously considered whether the service should not be reduced to three days a week, as there is no traffic to justify more'. The attached guard's report showed that, due to lack of traffic, the trains ran consistently ahead of time. According to railway historian John Thomas 'coal from Fife was the NBR's lifeblood' and on 23rd June an enquiry was made of William Arnott, the district traffic superintendent at Burntisland as to what he was doing to improve traffic on the line and in his reply he stated that,

> The traffic on this branch has not increased as we could have wished, and what we have got is principally traffic which formerly was dealt with at stations on the Leven & East of Fife line. The gradients on the East Fife Central are very heavy and as we have only a third class engine on the train it can only take equal to sixteen wagons of goods from Leven to East of Fife Central line.

Arnott went on to say that there would be no real saving in making the service only run on alternate days and that there might also be a public outcry if the daily train was withdrawn since during the winter months the up trains usually ran well loaded and that on occasions a special trip had to be made between Leven and Montrave. Stewart, however, was unconvinced that a daily service was required, stating that 'it is not incumbent upon the Railway Company to throw away money to give a daily service, when the traffic does not justify it'.

The matter of the frequency of service was settled, at least for the time being by a letter dated 5th July and written by Arnott who stated that he had been making enquiries and that if trains were to run only every second day then this would have a serious effect on the traffic of the Largoward Coal Co. who loaded coal at Largoward:

> The loading bank only admits to loading 7 wagons until they get a shunt and they can load that number each day. In about three weeks they will be able to load double that and they are asking us to provide increased loading accommodation. In these circumstances, I am afraid that we can scarcely curtail the service. This is practically the only additional traffic the line has brought us.

The loading banks were not the only improvement carried out at Largoward for on 9th November, 1900 the North British Minutes record that the tender had been approved in the sum of £296 19s. 7d. for the erection of the station agent's house - perhaps a good expenditure given that the building still survives to the present day! Further agreements were concluded with the Fife Lime Co. of Leven for a siding at Montrave in the sum of £300 and a station agent's house was approved by the NBR Board in the sum of £322 0s. 8d. on 19th December, 1901.

Perhaps the *Leven Advertiser* of 27th December summed up the rather bleak situation:

NOT AS EXPECTED 31

Coal has not been found in sufficient quantities to justify the opening up of any major collieries and beyond a conveyance of the requirements of an agricultural community, it cannot be said that of the railway that it is to be anything of a success.

One interesting working in 1901 was a special train operated on behalf of Sir John Gilmour, a member of the Fife Hunt, on Saturday 28th September:

101 Special Train - Montrave to Perth

		am
Montrave	dep.	9.00
East Fife Central Junction	dep.	9.20
Cameron Bridge	dep.	9.26
Thornton	pass	10.00
Bridge of Earn	dep.	10.30
Perth	arr.	10.40

Engine guard and van to work this special will leave Thornton at 7.30 am for Montrave. Note: Conveys Sir John Gilmour's horses (12 horse boxes).

Guarantors in trouble

From an early stage it was clear that the East Fife Central Railway was not going to pay its way. The mere fact that the North British had demanded guarantees from the hapless promoters of the East Fife Central and the failure to progress with the lines to Dairsie and Stravithie made this even more obvious and the disappointments over coal at Lochty meant that the one line which was built would never reach its potential. The total capital expenditure on the line from East of Fife Central Junction to Lochty, up to November 1899, amounted to £132,463 8s. 9d. - the estimated cost having been £104,820. In terms of the agreement between the two companies, the interest at 3 per cent on this sum for the 12 months up to 31st August, 1899 amounted to £3,973 18s. while the receipts within the same period amounted only to £1,124 4s. 8d. leaving a balance to be recovered from the guarantors of £2,849 13s. 4d. When the North British attempted to make the guarantors pay up there was a flurry of correspondence.

It was obvious that the guarantors were unhappy both with the financial position of the new line and also with the fact that they were now being asked to honour their guarantees which, it was generally felt, had not been entered into fairly and with the guarantors apparently being in possession of all the facts. In November 1899 John Jordan wrote to William Fulton Jackson, Wieland's protégé who had succeeded Conacher as General Manager of the North British, in terms that,

> No doubt you are aware that I never had any particular or pecuniary interest in the concern nominal holding of 40 shares necessary for a qualification, and I simply went into the matter in the interest of the North British Railway and at the desire of Mr Wieland who I should think will see that I am relieved of any responsibility.

One reason for Jordan's unhappiness was that he had been removed from the North British Board in March of that year by a Wieland-led cabal but Wieland's reply to an enquiry by Jackson stated that,

All that he [Jordan] states in his letter is quite true except that the Guarantee was not given in the interests of the North British Company but it would in my opinion be very hard indeed on him to pay - on the other hand the Company are in a delicate position – they have an agreement and may consider themselves bound to enforce it. I feel for Mr Jordan quite earnestly, but I should like to question if he means by his letter that I should personally relieve him or that I should represent his case to the Company for relief. I myself had no pecuniary or other interest in the railway,* although it went through some land I owned and should never have had anything to do with it but for the insistence of the promoters in soliciting my help.

Further correspondence ensued and in December of that year Wieland wrote directly to Jordan that,

I am at a complete loss to understand why I should relieve you of responsibility. There was not the faintest undertaking expressed or implied that I should do so, and I had no more interest than, as a Director of the North British, you had, in the making of the Railway. That it was made so you very properly say in the interests of the North British Company and to open up the Mineral Fields of the District, it is quite true, but that would not justify one Director in assuming the responsibility of another Director, simply because one happens to remain a Director of the Company and another does not ... It is very unfortunate for all of us, and I quite sympathise with your case and with that of the others, and of course not least with my own, but there is our Bond to preach us the lesson of our folly in undertaking at any time any obligation the extent of which we hadn't the sagacity to examine into and to realise.

Other guarantors complained that they, too, had been unaware of the extent of their financial indebtedness, a good example being Major-General Briggs who claimed that they had been told *on all sides* that the amounts they had expected to pay were nominal and that the sum spent on the line (and thus the capital upon which the 3 per cent would be payable) would not have exceeded £100,000.

In April 1900 an NBR committee which included Howard (hardly a disinterested party) decided that the guarantees, which had been outstanding and still in force for five years, should be discharged in the following sums: Jordan £1,600, Baxter £1,600, Wieland £1,600, Earl of Crawford £1,280, Sir Alexander Moncrieff £280, Major General Briggs £500 under the joint guarantee and £278 under a separate guarantee. Baxter and Briggs were to get credit for the sums already paid by them, provided that all of the guarantors agreed to such an agreement. There was, however, still a dispute as to what sums should be paid and at the end of that year it appeared that negotiations were still proceeding. What then happened is not clear. In one of those annoying terse NBR Minutes it is reported that on 8th August, 1901 that an agreement between the NBR and the guarantors was ordered to be sealed. The Chairman of the Board, and of the meeting, was now no other than G.B. Wieland, one of the guarantors, who had not yet paid a single penny. On 31st October the company solicitor wrote to Jackson returning his papers and stating that 'the matter is now settled'.

---

* A statement somewhat at odds with Wieland's speculative purchase of the Letham estate!

Chapter Four

Coal to the Rescue?: The North British Era Continued

'To facilitate business, extensive railway sidings are in the course of construction ...'
East of Fife Record, 26th January, 1911

The Baldastard Colliery

One of the principal reasons why the East Fife Central was built was to exploit the coal resources of the area to be served and although there was a sprinkling of existing small mines around the villages of New Gilston, Woodside and Largoward it was thought that the generally rising demand for coal and the imagined mineral riches of the district made the line an attractive proposition. In Dron's *Coalfields of Scotland*, published in 1902, it was said that,

> The splint coal, known as the Largoward Splint Coal ... has been more extensively worked than any other seams. On Lathallan estate a pit was sunk to the depth of 80 fathoms [480 ft] and all the coal available from that sinking worked out. While the pit was working, the output was about 200 tons per day, and this was disposed of by cart sale.

This coal would likely have been sold to the occupants of cottages, houses and local farms. It is probable that some coal from local mines may have been used to fire local limekilns and the boilers of small textile mills in the Cupar area. Prior to the construction of the line, coal was also carted down to the sea at Largo pier for coastal shipment and the carters would often return with loads of seaweed for use as fertiliser. Although Lathallan Colliery was closed in 1899, a colliery was opened in May 1898 at Baldastard, between Montrave and Largoward stations; within two months the Baldastard Colliery and Fireclay Co. had entered into an agreement with the North British for the construction of a siding to serve the pit at a cost of £423 3s. 8d., labour being paid for by the coal company who were also to pay interest at 4½ per cent on the value of the permanent way materials used. This siding, known as the Baldastard Colliery Siding, was situated 1 mile 51 chains east of Montrave station and was completed by September of that year. The Baldastard Colliery consisted of two pits and the works were described in a contemporary report* in the following terms,

> There is a winding engine and a pumping engine with three boilers built in and a chimney stalk erected at the main pit ... close to which most of the buildings for a brickwork are also ready, including a four-chambered continuous kiln with chimney, drying shed, machine house and engine house and workshops and there is an office and house for the manager and a short siding is put in alongside the railway, for the accommodation of the works on which a good deal of money has been expended.

The expenditure was, unfortunately, in vain for the Baldastard Colliery was bedevilled with flooding and closed early on, and the siding went out of use some time between 1902 and 1904. The NBR *List of Goods Stations, Sidings etc.* of 1st November, 1902 lists the siding but it may actually have been out of use by then and

---
* Report on Baldastard mineral field, Fife by Landale, Frew & Gemmell, August 1900.

Baldastard Colliery seen from the west, 1898.　　　　　　　　　　　　　　　　　　*John Howard*

Balcarres Colliery at Largoward, *circa* 1903.　　　　　　　　　　　　　　　　　*Authors' Collection*

the 17th June, 1904 supplement thereto shows it of having been closed - it did not survive long enough to ever having been shown on any Ordnance Survey map. The number of persons employed at Baldastard was stated to be as follows:

Year	Below ground	Above ground	Total
1898	17	4	21
1899	2	1	3
1900		'standing'	

There is no record of the Baldastard Colliery & Fireclay Co. ever having operated any railway wagons of its own or of its operating a 'pug' or shunting engine and accordingly any shunting would have been done by the North British branch engine or by horse.

The Largoward Coal Co.

Another early pit was that of the Largoward Coal Co. who operated the Balcarres Colliery, alternatively known as Cassingray Colliery, between Largoward and Lochty. The company was not limited but a partnership with the sole partner listed as Robert Ure, a solicitor of 81 Bath Street, Glasgow and latterly of 3 Rathelpie, St Andrews. This pit first appears in the Home Office list of mines for 1900 (although listed erroneously as the Largoward *Colliery* Company), and eventually a siding was constructed at the Balcarres (or Cassingray) Colliery, 1 mile 68 chains east of Largoward station and on the south side of the line in implementation of a memorandum of agreement between the North British and the coal company dated 21st February, 1901. The siding was constructed at the expense of the railway company, the Largoward company being responsible for paying the cost of the labour estimated at £354 and annual interest at the rate of 4½ per cent on the value of the permanent way (estimated at £999). The siding was used by the Largoward Coal Company's own fleet of private owner wagons, and indeed the company was the only trader on the East Fife Central known to have used its own wagons. A fleet of 40 wagons was registered with the North British and these were constructed by Hurst, Nelson and the Motherwell Wagon & Rolling Stock Co. of Lanarkshire. They consisted of two batches, namely Motherwell Nos. 21 to 40 (registration plates Nos. 16381 to 164000), put into service on 16th July, 1903, and Hurst, Nelson Nos. 1 to 20 (16401 to 16420) put into service on 6th November, 1903. Both batches were identical, having 10-ton wooden bodies with spring buffers and they appear to have been finished in a red oxide livery with the single legend 'LARGOWARD' appearing on each side; only one photograph of these wagons is known to exist, that shown in a post card image of Leven docks.* The Motherwell company ceased trading in the 1930s and its archives have not survived.† Once again there is no indication of the Largoward company owning any shunting locomotives.

---

* This is the image reproduced at p.128 of the authors' *Leven & East of Fife Railway*, (Oakwood Press, 2013).
† Unlike those of its two main Scottish rivals, R.Y. Pickering and Hurst, Nelson; unfortunately the official photographs of the Largoward wagons built by the latter seem to have become lost.

The band of the 6th Argyll & Sutherland Highlanders at their summer camp at Largoward with NBR rolling stock clearly visible in the background, July 1910.   *Alan Brotchie Collection*

A Fife Coal Company private owner wagon at Largoward six years after after nationalization of the coal industry, July 1953.   *George Ellis*

COAL TO THE RESCUE? 37

Between 1900 and 1905 the number of persons working at Balcarres/Cassingray was, according to the Home Office statistics, as follows:

Year	Below ground	Above ground	Total
1900	44	13	57
1901	63	13	76
1902	28	8	36
1903	58	8	66
1904	55	12	67
1905	60	13	73

In the year ending 31st January, 1905 Balcarres shipped 3,859 tons via Methil docks, 1,123 via Burntisland and 925 via other docks. By 1905 the colliery had passed to another concern known as the Carnbee and Kilconquhar Coal Co. but the pit was in trouble with severe problems caused by excess water underground. It ceased production shortly afterwards, the Carnbee company being wound up on 31st March, 1906, and the Balcarres Colliery Siding is shown in the December 1906 supplement to the North British list of sidings as being closed.

Limping on

The first decade of the century was not a good one for the East Fife Central as coal mines came and went and much of the anticipated minerals and other traffic failed to materialize. The four public goods depots did, however, survive. At Kennoway the adjacent gas works received some inward coal supplies by rail and, latterly, the Wemyss Coal Co. rented space there for a coal depot as a distribution point for local coal merchants such as Hendersons. The majority of the traffic here was, however, agricultural in nature. At Montrave, traffic was wholly agricultural and was augmented by bloodstock traffic for Sir John Gilmour. A mile away was the Teasses limeworks which, although not directly rail served, does appear to have provided traffic at Montrave via carting. The Teasses Lime Co., who owned the mine and worked it on the stoup and room method, abandoned the site by 1939. At Largoward, where a station master's house was also erected, traffic included seed potatoes, and flax from the Earl of Crawford's farms destined for Blairgowrie. Several small pits in the area, principally Thomas Brown & Company's Largoward Colliery and the small Lathones pit were all producing coal at this time in the vicinity but little of this travelled by rail; what did was normally carted to Largoward station amounting in total to between 1,500 and 4,900 tons annually. Finally there was Lochty, the terminus literally situated in the middle of nowhere, which dealt with agricultural traffic and inward coal. This station was even more ramshackle than the intermediate ones and consisted of an old coach body serving as an office and bothy, several sidings, a loading bank and 2-ton crane, and a house for the station master. It lay adjacent to the country road which gave access to a large number of farms on the upland part of the East Neuk. Kennoway and Montrave also had 2-ton cranes while Largoward had a 1½ ton crane.

The North British did what they could to attract new custom but there was little demand for a railway that wound its leisurely way through a quiet and largely undeveloped area and managed to avoid any real centres of population and industry. Had local farms not been so productive it is doubtful if the line would have survived more than a handful of years but one innovation was the only private siding for agricultural use, which opened in about 1912* at Letham Farm, two miles east of Kennoway station. The siding, which had a loading bank, was put in to serve Letham Farm and constructed at an estimated cost of £300 paid by the Fife Coal Company, the farm being tenanted by the firm of Robert and Alexander Kerr whose landlord was the Fife Coal Co. who owned the mineral rights in the area. These included the Kilmux pit which, at one time, saw a small amount of outward traffic carted by road to the siding.

Territorial trains

In the summer of 1910 in the fields in the vicinity of Largoward station large Territorial Army camps were held for a number of weeks and arrangements were made with the North British to convey various detachments, including a battalion of the 6th Argyll & Sutherland Highlanders to and from the camp by rail. Because it was intended to open the line to passenger traffic, albeit of a limited nature, it was necessary to obtain sanction from the Railway Inspectorate before this could be done. On 18th July, 1910 Major Pringle of the Inspectorate reported that the North British wished to use the line as far as Largoward goods loop for a period of four weeks for the troop trains:

> The loop and siding points between the junction and Largoward are worked by single line padlocked dwarf frames and these are also provided with trap points which lay normally for the dead ends. For troop trains the line was to be worked by a pilotman and staff in accordance (where possible) with the precautions detailed in General Rules 227 *et seq.* ... All points and connections on the through road to be wedged and cramped [*sic*] ... If the gradients on the single line east of Largoward falls from east to west at an incline steeper than 1 in 240, a set of hand worked catch points (to work as runaway or trap points) must be provided outside the east and west loop points at Largoward...

The railway was used to transport the men, their horses and equipment including large tanks of water since it had been found that the Largoward site suffered from a lack of available drinking water. The special railway arrangements were a great success but were never repeated.

Largobeath Colliery

The final and most easterly pit with rail connection to the East Fife Central was the Largobeath Colliery, situated 21 chains east of the Balcarres Siding. Largobeath was also confusingly known as Cassingray Colliery, but separate from the earlier Balcarres/Cassingray Colliery referred to above. On 26th January, 1911 the *East of Fife Record* reported that,

> Rapid progress is being made with the development of the new Largoward coalfield, owned by the East of Fife Coal Company Limited. The sinking contractors, Messrs Addie, at a depth of 40 fathoms, have struck what is termed the 'real Largoward Splint'.

---

* The NBR Works Committee Minutes of 3rd March, 1910 refer to a plan for the siding and it is shown on a plan dated 14th November, 1912.

COAL TO THE RESCUE? 39

The seam is four feet in thickness. Two analyses have been taken, the results of which prove it to be of a very rare and rich quality of parlour coal, the percentage of ash being very low. Mining experts claim it to be superior in many respects to the 'Dunfermline Splint'. At a further depth of 12 fathoms to reach the seam, 5 fathoms are already sunk. During the erection of a massive pithead frame and permanent winding engine, sinking operations were suspended for a short time. A resumption, however, has now been made and it is anticipated that a month hence coal will be winding its way to the surface. Spacious offices, along with the general workshops have been erected. The screening plant, including the erection of the pithead work, when complete, will be on the most up-to-date principles. To facilitate business, extensive railway sidings are in the course of construction, and will soon be completed. The siding will join the present existing East of Fife North British mineral line.

The East of Fife Coal Co. was a Glasgow concern incorporated in January 1911 and its Directors were all members of the Symington family. The Symingtons were also connected to another business which had undertaken railway construction work, namely Hugh Symington & Sons Ltd. According to the Home Office returns a workforce at Largobeath Colliery reaching a total of 85 below ground and 25 above was employed. Initially the coal traffic was deemed to be successful and it appears that enough coal was produced to justify a single eight hour shift being worked each weekday over a period of several months. However the optimism that resulted in the opening of the Largobeath Colliery proved to be short-lived and once again the life of the pit was limited, the mine being abandoned in June 1914 after production ceased following persistent difficulties with inrushes of water from the nearby abandoned workings at the old Balcarres Colliery. The workforce was dismissed and the almost new equipment was put up for sale by auction. The East of Fife Coal Co. ceased all trading in 1916 and was subsequently removed from the Register of Companies.

Passengers arrive and depart

From the railway point of view, however, the most interesting factor was that there was a private passenger service run over the East Fife Central line for the benefit of the workforce at the Largobeath pit. The service was required because there was an insufficient number of miners living locally for the requirements of the new mine and additional labour was accordingly needed from elsewhere. To make it practical for men to travel to work from the Windygates/Methilhill/Leven area to Largobeath Colliery, a special service was provided from Cameron Bridge station from 1st February, 1913. This had been authorized by the Board of Trade when on 10th January of that year Major Pringle reported that,

> Single line platforms have been provided at Kennoway and at Largobeath Colliery Siding, and the loop points at the undermentioned places have been fitted with facing point locks and worked from a ground frame each containing 2 levers locked by a key on the train staff: Kennoway (loop) 2 frames, Letham (siding) 1 frame, Montrave (loop) 2 frames, Largoward (loop) 2 frames. The interlocking is correct and subject to a speed limit of 25 mph and the adoption of the method of One Engine in Steam carrying the train staff between East Fife Central Junction and Largobeath Colliery Platform, the platform can be used by workmen's trains of suitable length.

There were two trains per day, an outward working to Largobeath in the early morning and a return working mid-afternoon. The service ran as follows,

		am A	am B			pm B	pm A	pm B
Cameron Bridge	dep.	5.15		Lochty	dep.	1.25		
Leven	dep.		11.20	Largobeath Colliery	dep.	1.40	2.30	
East Fife Central Jn	arr.	5.18		Largoward	arr.	1.50	2.33	4.20
	dep.	5.22	11.25	Montrave	dep.		2.45	4.45
Kennoway	dep.	5.27	11.40	Kennoway	dep.		2.58	5.10
Montrave	dep.	5.39	12.05	East Fife Central Jn	arr.		3.03	5.15
Largoward	dep.	5.51	12.35		dep.		3.07	5.20
Largobeath Colliery	dep.	5.54	1.00	Cameron Bridge	arr.		3.10	5.25
Lochty	arr.	C	1.10					

A - Workmen, B - East Fife Mineral, C - Engine, guard and van return at once to Thornton

The colliery workers were conveyed to and from their eight-hour shift on Mondays to Fridays and on alternate Saturdays from 8th February and stock of their train was probably made up of two or three NBR vintage four-wheeled carriages dating from the 1870s. The speed of the workmen's trains was limited to 25 mph and the weekly cost to passengers for their short journeys was likely to have been a matter of pennies.

At Kennoway a wooden passenger platform for the use of these trains was built, 118 ft long, 8 ft broad and 3 ft in height with two oil-lit lamps on posts and situated on the down side close to the south end of the loop. The halt* had no building, shelter or name board since it was not open to the public and although it went out of use shortly thereafter the remains of the platform survived right into the 1950s. The Largobeath platform was similar,† being 120 ft in length and situated on the down side west of the junction with the colliery sidings; there was no shelter provided and it is likely that it, too, was lit by oil-lamps.

The service ceased to operate within a few months and the North British working timetable dated 1st December, 1913 contained the entry that 'The 5.15 am workmen's train from Cameron Bridge to Largobeath has been discontinued', its demise being directly attributable to the severe water problems which stopped coal production and eventually doomed the colliery. It may well have been thought (or hoped) that these problems would be of a temporary nature for the 1914 North British General Appendix still contained the following entry:

> Workmen's Trains between East Fife Central Junction and Largobeath: The speed of trains containing workmen between East Fife Central Junction and Largobeath must not exceed 25 miles per hour.

The Largobeath miners' trains and the Territorials' troop trains were the only known instances of any passenger trains on the line and, apart from a few enthusiasts' brake van trips prior to closure, there were apparently no other such trains despite some erroneous published claims to the contrary.

---

* Shown on National Archives of Scotland plan RHP 15909.
† See RHP 15910.

The Kaiser's War and its aftermath

With the closure of the Largobeath Colliery the line reverted to its mainly agricultural role and the daily goods service was nominally operated on six days per week. Kennoway, Largoward and Lochty stations still remained staffed notwithstanding World War I withdrawal of nearby passenger traffic and the reduced goods traffic at nearby stations such as Pittenweem and Mount Melville. Probably the reason for the Lochty line stations remaining open was the Government's determination to keep home food production at a high level to try to beat the German U-boat blockade of British merchant shipping, together with the fact that these stations were only staffed by a single railwayman without assistance. The amount of traffic at these stations also increased and the immediate post-war boom saw increased tonnages handled and the highest ever income received in the closing years of the North British era. As a sad coda to the North British era the *East of Fife Observer* of 2nd June, 1921 carried the following:

The death took place on Wednesday last of Mr David Dobson, late station agent, Lochty. Deceased, who only retired from Lochty station last December, had been suffering from the result of two nasty accidents he had received in the last few months of his service on the railway ... Mr Dobson was a very well known and respected public servant of a kind and extremely obliging disposition which endeared him to all he came in contact with.

EAST FIFE CENTRAL RAILWAY — Week-days.

UP TRAINS. Stations and Sidings.	Distance from East Fife Central Junc.		1	2	3	4
	M.	C.	Min.	Min.		
Departs from .. {			Leven a.m. 11 20	Leven 11a20	...	...
East Fife Cen. Jc. dep.	...	...	TO FO TF 11a25	TO FO 11a25	...	...
Kennoway ,,	1	27	11 40	11 40		
Montrave ,,	6	4	12 5	12 5	...	...
Largoward ,,	10	64	12 40	12 40		
Largobeath Colliery ,,	11	73	......	......	...	...
Lochty ... ... arr.	14	50	12 55	Stop.	......	......

DOWN TRAINS. Stations and Sidings.	Distance from Lochty.		1	2	3	4
	M.	C.	Min.	Min.		
Lochty ... ... dep.	...	...	TO FO p.m.	TF 1p15	...	...
Largobeath Colliery ,,	2	57	...	...	......	......
Largoward ,,	3	66	1 0	1 40	...	...
Montrave ,,	8	46	1 35	2 15	......	......
Kennoway ,,	13	23	2 5	2 45	...	...
East Fife Cen. Junc. arr.	14	50	2 15	2 55	......	......
Arrives at destination {	...	...	Camer on Br. 2 28	Camer on Br. 3 8	...	...

NBR working timetable showing the reduced wartime service, May 1918.

EAST FIFE CENTRAL RAILWAY.
20th Sept. 1926   105
WEEK-DAYS.

UP TRAINS. Stations and Sidings.	Distance from East Fife Central Junc.		1	2 Min. Leven a.m. 11 20 TO ThO SO	3	4	DOWN TRAINS. Stations and Sidings.	Distance from Lochty.		1	2 Min. Leven a.m. 11 20 TO ThO SO	3	4
Departs from ..					...	...	Departs from ...					...	...
	M.	C.		a.m.				M.	C.		p.m.		
East Fife Cen. Jc. dep.	...	...	...	11 40	...	...	Lochty ... dep.	...	...	...	1 45	...	...
Kennoway ,,	1	27		12 0	...	......	Largoward ,,	3	66		2 5	...	......
Letham Siding ,,	3	78	...	...	...	...	Montrave ,,	8	46	......	2 40	......	......
Montrave ,,	6	4	...	12 35	......	......	Kennoway ,,	13	23	...	3 10	...	......
Largoward ,,	10	64	......	1 10	......	......	East Fife Cen. Junc. arr.	14	50	...	3 20	...	......
Lochty ... arr.	14	50	......	1 25	......	......							
Arrives at ... {				Thornton Jc. 6‡0	......	......	Arrives at ... {				Thornton Jc. 6‡0	...	...
‡ No. 2 Up and Down.—4-20 T O and Th O.													

LNER working timetable September 1926.

Kennoway station from a postcard view of the late 1920s. Note the houses newly built in Sandy Brae, the small NBR goods office, the Myreside overbridge and the interesting selection of rolling stock including open wagons from the LMS and the Lochgelly Iron & Coal Co. and, perhaps unusually, the 'foreign' box van from the Great Western Railway.   *Alan Brotchie Collection*

Chapter Five

Through the Buffers: The London & North Eastern Railway

'The engine had crashed through the buffer stops and ploughed its way through the embankment.'
Leven Advertiser, 14th November, 1939

Three times per week

Although the East Fife Central line changed visibly little during the LNER period, its fortunes were clearly in decline. By now the line was officially only open during daylight hours for safety reasons, there being no fixed signals except at the junction and at the goods yards and sidings there was no illumination for shunting or loading purposes other than hand-held oil lamps. The speed limit over the line was still 15 mph and by September 1926 the service over it was being operated on Tuesdays, Thursdays and Saturdays only with a single service from Thornton which passed East Fife Central Junction at 11.40 am, reaching Kennoway at 12 noon, Montrave at 12.35, Largoward at 1.10 and arriving at Lochty at 1.25 pm. Leaving Lochty at 1.45 pm, the train called at Largoward at 2.05, Montrave at 2.40, Kennoway at 3.10 and passing East Fife Central Junction at 3.20 pm - this train continued to run to virtually the same timings and hauled by the same locomotives for another 40 years! Given that the tonnages of goods carried and the concomitant revenues that the line generated were all in decline, it is perhaps curious that the whole of the line was not closed as part of the LNER retrenchment carried out in the depression years of the early 1930s but there are perhaps several reasons why this was so. The line was still a useful feeder of traffic to the rest of the system and in particular after the sugar beet factory at Cupar was opened in 1926 there was heavy traffic in the all too brief beet season.* Seed potato traffic also became prominent on the line but once again a deteriorating economic situation helped to keep traffic to a modest level such that the branch was barely managing to generate enough revenue to earn its keep.

Another factor was that there would have been little commercial reason for closing the line particularly since it had no passenger service over it and, so long as no major capital expenditure was needed to keep the goods trains operating, closure would be seen as a major blow for the already struggling farmers in the area. Whether or not the influence of Sir John Gilmour, the second baronet and Minister of Agriculture, was influential is, however, debatable. Perhaps the LNER had forgotten the line altogether or the losses that it made were minimal and the lightly used trackwork needed little capital expenditure.

Declining fortunes

Perhaps the most significant factor, however, in the declining fortunes of the line was the rise of the motor tractor and lorry. In an era when the horse was the only

---

* The factory was opened on 11th December by Lady Gilmour of Montrave and was owned by the Second Anglo-Scottish Sugar Beet Company Ltd - see further 'The Beet Generation - Sugar Beet in Fife' by Wynne Hartley published in *Historic Scotland*, January/February 2003.

available means of transport there was little reason for local farmers not to rely on the branch line to transport agricultural produce and requisites, livestock and coal. But the Lochty line was already becoming a victim of competition from the internal combustion engine. Motor lorries, and those possessing the ability to drive them, became increasingly commonplace as a result of World War I and the cheap availability of army surplus vehicles and those who were familiar with using them became a feature of the local scene. By the early 1920s, and more so after the disruptions of the General Strike of 1926, together with the increasing ability of such vehicles to carry heavier loads more economically as well as their ability to carry goods without the necessity for transhipment, the motor lorry became an ever increasing threat to the once profitable monopoly enjoyed by the railway. Not only did a number of local carriers improve their provision of services to local farmers but the farmers themselves began to buy tractors with trailers and even small lorries for their own use. An example of local carters entering into competition with the railway was the firm of M.B. Danskin of Strathkinness near to St Andrews and whose trade flourished to such an extent that they established a branch in Colinsburgh in the 1930s and, specializing in transport business from farms and factories, began to take away traffic from the Lochty line.

All local goods stations show a significant decline in their cash takings between 1913 and 1933 and the tonnage of coal and other minerals showed a sharp decline over this period. This was commensurate with the national economic situation and the continuing fall in demand for coal on farms with the advent of the petrol engine and, towards the end of the period, by the coming of rural electric power. The railway tried hard, however, to retain as much of the general goods traffic as it could, ignoring the fact that it was becoming increasingly unprofitable to handle the same. Livestock shipped locally showed up in a slight increase in traffic figures, particularly at Largoward which became an increasingly important local railhead for this traffic as well as for the transit of produce and the distribution of coal from the collieries at Leven and Weymss. Attempts were made to reduce costs by reducing manpower and on 1st July, 1927 the goods office at Kennoway was closed, the staff from Cameron Bridge being used to handle all traffic to and from Kennoway.

Attempts to encourage traffic

In 1930 a further source of traffic was provided when the Radernie Colliery Co. Ltd at Radernie, situated near to the village of Peat Inn, was opened in May 1930. Although not directly rail-served, coal was carted to Largoward station for onward transit by rail to Methil Docks for export and the pit employed between 30 and 50 men at times. On 12th July, 1946 the pit was, however, closed when the Ministry of Fuel and Power, who were responsible for directing the coal industry at the time, decreed that the two parallel drift mines of Radernie would be closed so that its miners could be directed to the larger and more productive pits in the Wemyss areas. During the immediate pre-nationalization period considerable quantities of timber (tree trunks) were hauled by rail up the branch to be stored at Lochty on behalf of the Wemyss Sawmills of James Donaldson & Sons at Leven. The Fife Paper Mills Ltd of Leven, who operated the Millfield Paper Mill, obtained a supply of coal for their boiler house from the small pits remaining in the Largoward area and this traffic travelled by rail from Largoward. It was said that these pits owed their continuing existance to the fact that they were worked by miners who had been 'black listed' by the Weymss Coal Co. and the Fife Coal Co. for playing a prominent part in the 1926 General Strike.

Before World War II further attempts were made to find coal at Lochty and experimental boring was carried out to the south of the station there in July 1936. A seven foot coal seam was found* but subsequent borings established that its exploitation could not be viably undertaken - further unsuccessful attempts to find commercially viable mined seams were undertaken as late as 1955.

Untypical events

An unusual incident on the line occurred during the May 1926 General Strike when an Anstruther to Edinburgh passenger train was diverted unexpectedly onto the Lochty line owing to a malefactor having tampered with the points at East Fife Central Junction.† Another incident was reported thus in the *Leven Advertiser & Wemyss Gazette* of 14th November, 1939:

> RAILWAY ENGINE ON FIFE ROAD
> Maintenance and permanent way men were engaged on Wednesday removing a goods locomotive from the public road at Lochty, five miles west of Crail. The engine had crashed through the buffer stops and ploughed its way through the embankment on to the main road which was blocked. Traffic had to detour eight miles by way of St Andrews or Anstruther. The mishap occurred when the locomotive was shunting in thick fog. The impact was so great that the embankment was pushed in front of the engine, across the road and the locomotive came to rest with its front buffer beam a few inches from the fence on the far side. With the assistance of two engines from the depot the derailed locomotive was pulled back on to the embankment and the road cleared. Efforts continued until late to jack up the engine on to the permanent way.

The press photograph showed the locomotive at the side of the road rather than across it – since there was in any event no embankment at this point the newspaper reports seem to have been somewhat exaggerated. The derailed locomotive involved was 'J37' class 0-6-0 No. 9139 (latterly BR No. 64559) and the depot from where assistance came was, of course, Thornton.

In the severe winter of 1947 (the last winter prior to nationalization) deep snow affected the line on a number of occasions. This culminated in an event when the line was completely blocked by deep snow which had accumulated during a prolonged blizzard and an engine fitted with a snowplough was completely stuck in the drift. This led to a breakdown crew being summoned along with three locomotives, two 'J36' 0-6-0s and one 'J37' 0-6-0, being coupled together to propel a snow plough to clear the blockage.

Local life

An account of branch line life in the 1930s was provided by a local railway employee, the late J.M. Bennett, in his 1975 work *Random Reflections of a Roving Railman,* where he states that,

> In March 1936 I was appointed Station Master at Largoward, dropping in salary from £170 to £160 per annum for this *privilege*. After living in the village lodging with Mr and

---

* *Leven Advertiser* 28th July, 1936.
† The incident is dealt with in *The Leven and East of Fife Railway,* p.147.

Mrs Duff, Briarlea Cottage, for six months I got married and took over the Station House. Living conditions were somewhat primitive with a dry toilet at the bottom of the garden. For drinking water we had to rely on two small barrels which made alternate journeys from Cameron Bridge by the Goods train which ran three days a week from Thornton yard. Only once I think did we run short and had to await the arrival of the train before lunch could be prepared.

Mr Bennett went on to relate that the station master at Montrave was Caesar Smith, an old school friend of his and that they frequently visited each other. Largoward was an apparently social place to live and the duties of the 'Stationie' seemed to include acting as referee in a local football match as well as handling the heavy potato and grain traffic at the station. The local coal merchant, Edgar Cowell, spent each morning at the station but in the afternoon attended to his other occupation as a repairer of boots and shoes, leaving Mr Bennett to deal with the coal traffic for which he received from Mr Cowell a commission of 6d. for each cartload handled.

During World War II proposals were put forward in June 1943 to greatly increase the siding capacity at Kennoway to accommodate 20 additional wagons and a further 50 wagons on sidings to be laid in due course - the necessity for this was apparently based on the demands of wartime traffic but for whatever reason the proposed sidings were never built.

A very poor quality image of a rare visitor biting the dust - 'J37' class No. 9139 ends up through the fence at Lochty, November 1939 in this *Leven Advertiser* picture. Rerailed, this engine survived for another 24 years. *Authors' Collection*

Chapter Six

Infrequent Appearances: The British Railways Era

'The farmer ... was taking potatoes from one field across the railway line where the slow moving goods train ... made one of its infrequent appearances.'
Leven Mail, 15th November, 1961

Miscellaneous goods

The story of the steady decline in the fortunes of the Lochty branch after nationalization is mirrored by the inexorable general decline in railway goods traffic throughout Britain. 'Fife, like the rest of the country, would welcome the proposed co-ordination of the various transport industries, provided that it was not achieved at too great an overall cost' as *The Third Statistical Account of Scotland, County of Fife* said in 1952 but by then the early promise of effective state control of road haulage was not implemented. The abolition of the common carrier obligations on British Railways (BR) and the general increase in the number of lorries and farm trailers in Fife brought about a further decrease in agricultural traffic by rail. After the disastrous effects of the ASLEF strike in 1955 practically the only remaining goods traffic on the branch was that of wagon loads from the county's coalfields bringing in fuel for local needs and a small amount of outward sugar beet and miscellaneous goods whose transport had not been priced away by the increasingly loss-making Scottish Region goods managers. Inevitably the local goods stations attracted less and less traffic and with effect from 2nd May, 1957 Kennoway station was reclassified as an unstaffed public siding from April to September each year. This left only local staff employed at Montrave, Largoward and Lochty although latterly not on a full-time basis. Further retrenchment occurred with effect from 6th February, 1961 when these stations were similarly classified and thus all branch-based staff were now withdrawn. These partial closures did merit some discussion by the Wemyss Local Committee of the Fife County Council when there was talk about extra road traffic that might be generated but, as at least one councillor pointed out, the decision had apparently already been taken by local businesses having long ago forsaken the railway and there was little point in the Council expressing any opposition at this stage.

A rural backwater

Whereas it was true that little had been done to modernize the branch line in the last 50 years it was difficult to see what could have been done to encourage traffic. The stations when staffed had few facilities and it was said that living conditions there were primitive, Lochty having no running water and dry toilets situated at the end of the garden with drinking water being brought by train from Thornton in wooden barrels. One curious factor was that although Kennoway was supervised by the Cameron Bridge station master, Lochty, Largoward and Montrave all came under the jurisdiction of the Kilconquhar station master and in order that he could carry out these duties, he was provided with a small motorcycle, there being no public transport to link the branch sidings with his home station.

47

Lochty looking east towards the buffer stops, July 1953. *J.L. Stevenson*

An almost deserted Lochty station looking west, July 1953. *J.L. Stevenson*

Snowed up - two 'J36s' and a 'J37' in trouble at Knightsward in the famously cold winter of the first year of nationalization. *Authors' Collection*

The basic thrice-weekly summer train service was unaltered with a trip working from Thornton sufficing when required and although the line was animated with a small amount of general goods traffic in the winter, during the summer months traffic was so light that spare wagons were often stored in the sidings.

Montrave typically was used to handle local seed potato traffic which was destined for the south and when this traffic was dealt with, normally between October to March, a porter from Cameron Bridge or Kennoway was sent to supervise the loading of the 8 ton closed vans which were lined with straw and covered in a tarpaulin to prevent frost damage. Wagons were normally loaded in the afternoons and then picked up by the daily freight the next day. All stations still were busy with the beet campaign in October and November when the loaded open wagons were taken to Cupar. By the early 1960s the coal traffic had dwindled to a few winter deliveries and therefore the beet and seed potatoes were now all that kept the branch open while summer traffic, never great in quantity, was by then almost non-existent.

Untoward events

The Lochty branch was rarely in the news and two incidents merely served to underline the quiet nature of this rural by-way. In December 1960 a 16-year-old Methil youth was fined £2, with expenses of 28s. 0d., after he admitted at Kirkcaldy juvenile court that he had released a permanent way bogie which had been secured at Kennoway station and which then ran down the line before hitting the buffers at East Fife Central Junction. The prosecutor stated that had the points not been set for the stub line to the buffers the bogie could have run on to the main line and collided with a passenger train on the Fife Coast line; fortunately there was, apparently, little danger of the bogie colliding with one of the rare goods train on the Lochty line. Collisions with the latter were, however, not impossible and the *Leven Mail* of 15th November, 1961 carried the report of another incident:

> A 73-year old Fife farmer escaped death by seconds on Monday when the trailer of the tractor which he was drawing was hit by a passing train at a level crossing. It happened 400 yards from the train's next stop at Largoward. The farmer, Mr Richard Telford of Lathallan Home Farm, Kilconquhar, was taking potatoes from one field across the railway line to the potato pit in another field when the slow-moving goods train from Montrave to Lochty made one of its infrequent appearances at 1.15 in the afternoon. Potato gatherers in the fields and his two sons rushed to Mr Telford's aid when the engine caught the rear end of the trailer, spun the tractor right round, smashed the trailer in pieces and threw the driver over a fence into the field. He was treated by a doctor on the spot and taken home suffering from shock and severe bruising.

Another incident is mentioned by Westwater and Page in their book on the Lochty Private Railway, *The First Ten Years*, under the title 'The engine that nearly stuck in the snow':

> The following story was related to me some time ago by Mr Watson, a retired engine driver from Thornton MPD. On this occasion he was in charge of a 'J36' fitted with a small snow plough at the front for snow clearing duty on the Lochty branch. After the best part of a shift, spent ramming deep snowdrifts with the plough, with darkness falling they finally reached Lochty. As they were low on water they immediately set off

Snowed-up again! Another cold winter and two 'J36s' Nos. 65345 and 65253 derailed near
Largoward in February 1963. *Neil Woods*

No. 65253 being lifted by the Thornton steam crane. This engine, named *Joffre*, saw active service
in World War I but barely survived this incident, being withdrawn three months later.
Neil Woods

No. 65345 being rerailed by the steam crane.. *Neil Woods/Alan Brotchie Collection*

BR Standard class '4' 2-6-0 No. 76111 to the rescue.. *Neil Woods/Alan Brotchie Collection*

Shadows are cast by the photographers of 'J35' No. 64478 at Lochty, 20th January, 1962.
W.A. Camwell/Alan Brotchie Collection

No. 65345, one of the last 'J36s' to be built, at Montrave, 25th March, 1961. Note the station agent's house in the background. *Douglas Hume*

in reverse, however the snow was already drifting back across the line, and the engine became stuck a short way into the cutting. With no plough on the tender, ramming was useless.

He gave his young fireman, who had been 'cooried doon' in the corner of the cab, the following ultimatum: 'that he could walk back to East Fife Central Junction (14 miles), borrow the Lochty station master's bike and cycle to Anstruther to phone control for assistance or he could get the shovel off the tender and dig'. Rather sheepishly he dug.

It was a hard struggle from then on. By the time they reached Kennoway the tender tank was empty and the water was just showing in the gauge glass. Although it's down hill from there to East Fife Central he was worried in case they got delayed for this would have meant throwing out the fire for fear of blowing the fusible plug; that being regarded by enginemen as the 'cardinal sin'. Driver Watson assured me that he was never so relieved as he was then, when 'the bag' [water column] at Cameron Bridge hove in sight.

Another event mentioned in the same book was said to have occurred in the early 1950s when the brakes on the engine and brake van combined with the wet greasy rails of the 1 in 70 downward gradient were insufficient to stop the loose-coupled goods train and it ploughed through the buffers, demolishing the fence and ended up on the public road at Lochty with the wagons ending up in a heap in the goods yard. After a prolonged rainy spell the ground took a week to dry out before the breakdown crane could recover the 'J36'.

A windy Saturday

Goods traffic may have been vanishing but this obscure rural by-way with its splendid views over the countryside of a rarely visited part of Fife had an attraction for the railway enthusiast and a number of 'specials' operated over the branch from 1960 onwards. We are indebted to the late W.A.C. (Bill) Smith for his account of a 1961 journey on the line:

> On a cloudy, windy Saturday, 25th March, 1961, I joined a Branch Line Society party for a trip over the East Fife Central Railway, better known as the Lochty branch. The freight (daily in winter) was booked to leave Thornton old yard, opposite the North end of the passenger platform, at 11.15 am. The train consisted of 'J36' ex-NBR No. 65345 with a wagon of coal and three empty vanfits, a second brake van being attached to accommodate a party of eight. Departure was some five minutes early to cross the main line and go down the Coast line to rattle through Cameron Bridge, where a small Ruston & Hornsby diesel was shunting in the distillery sidings, and arrive at East Fife Central Junction at 11.25 am where we diverged into Kirkland yard and the loco ran round, being chimney first for the branch.
>
> After 'B1' No. 61146 had passed with the two-coach 10.46 from Crail we left the yard at 11.43 am, got the tablet at the box and took the branch to climb above the Thornton line and adjoining River Leven before passing under the A915 Cameron Bridge to Leven road and swinging away through cuttings. Continuing climbing, with screeching flanges, to face east again, we reached Kennoway at 11.54 am. In the sidings there were two wagons of coal, which were joined by the wagon we had brought from Thornton , and several empties. Continuing at 12.05 pm we left the valley below the village with the roof tops of Leven away to our right, and slowly wound across rolling, wooded country alternating between cuttings and embankments and passing Burnside Farm crossing, followed by rusting Letham siding, to arrive at lonely Montrave, set on a

Montrave station in its latter days. *Owen Duffy*

The crew stand beside 'J36' No. 65345 after shunting the goods at Lochty, 18th February, 1961.
W.S. Sellar

windswept hillside and with a view of the distant Firth, at 12.30 pm. The engine placed our three wagons in the sidings, joined by a pair already there, to await loading with seed potatoes by local farmers, and 'piece' time* followed.

No further traffic was on offer, but with the party having paid 13s. per head for the privilege of travelling to Lochty† the journey resumed at 1.04 pm for No. 65345 and the two brake vans to go down across the farmlands, bridging the Boghall Burn and passing what appeared to have been the site of sidings, then climbed along with Largo Law to the south and the site of the short branch coming in from the left from Baldastard Colliery, where the remains of buildings could be discerned; nearer Lochty, said the guard, there had been another colliery, Largobeath, also closed many years previously. Emerging from a shallow cutting, we then curved across a bleak countryside, the track on this section being rather grass-grown although with some relaying in progress, and swung down a wide curve into Largoward at 1.25, where a five-minute stop was made. Similar to Montrave, although with entrance to the sidings (containing two vans) from the west end, it had a loop which was occupied by stored wagons.

Leaving on an embankment, in occasional sunshine but into a near gale sweeping across the bare fields we dropped into Lochty, reaching it at 1.46. Situated just short of the B940 Crail to Cupar road, Lochty station was set in open country with little signs of habitation. Facilities comprised of a loop full of stored wagons, a couple of sidings serving a dilapidated loading bank and a weather-beaten coach body. The brake vans were gravity shunted and the return journey commenced at 1.59, Largoward being passed at 2.15 and Kennoway at 2.46 to Kirkland yard where the engine rounded and, passing a Metro-Cammell triple-set forming the 1.40 Edinburgh to Anstruther service followed by 'WD' class 2-8-0 No. 90575 on empty wagons, Thornton Junction was reached at 3.12, where No. 65345 detached the brake vans and departed for the MPD.

Death of a branch line

However, there was little financial justification for continuing operation of the delightful but moribund line and the fact that even the local coal traffic was deserting to the lorry made an early closure on economic grounds a certainty. Largoward was now the only station on the line that handled an average of more than five wagonloads of traffic per week and even these loadings, considerably less than the minimum figure of 5,000 tons considered to justify on economic grounds keeping even a single siding open, were in excess of the minimal traffic using the rest of the line. The branch line limped on, its thrice-weekly service provided by the now elderly North British locomotives being supplemented by occasional small diesel engines. After August 1962 there was apparently so little regular traffic on the easternmost section of the line between Largoward and Lochty that the former station became the virtual terminus of the line and Lochty itself was primarily used only as the storage point only of condemned wagons.

In the harsh winter of 1962-63 when the Rigging of Fife, in common with much of the rest of the country, became snowbound, considerable efforts were made to keep the line open. After two 'J36' class 0-6-0s, Nos. 65345 and 65253, coupled tender to tender with a snowplough in front of each locomotive became derailed near Largoward, due to the accumulation of hard packed snow and ice, the line was blocked for some two weeks following the unsuccessful attempt to clear the way with a breakdown crane which also became derailed. This had to be rescued by No. 76111, a BR Standard 2-6-0, a type of locomotive rarely seen on the line.

* Tea-break [authors].
† The decimal equivalent is 65p! In BR days it was possible to buy special tickets for pre-booked organized parties to travel over goods lines - this particular ticket was issued at Thornton and the fare was charged at the equivalent of the first-class mileage rate.

Arriving at Largoward, 18th February, 1961. *W.S. Sellar*

'J36' class 0-6-0 No. 65345 with the branch goods in March 1961 leaving Kennoway. The wooded hill in the background is none other than the famed Maiden Castle.

W.A.C. Smith/Transport Treasury

INFREQUENT APPEARANCES

Lochty railtour with 'J35' awaits passengers at Thornton Junction, 20th January, 1962.
Hamish Stevenson

Hunslet 0-6-0DM No. D2585 on the Lochty goods at Largoward, April 1963.
Hamish Stevenson Collection

Hunslet 0-6-0DM No. D2585 shunting at Lochty, April 1963.   *Hamish Stevenson Collection*

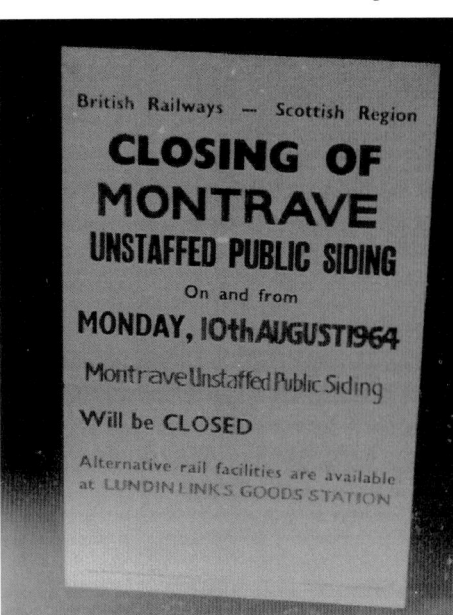

Closure notice, Montrave.   *Owen Duffy*

Closure notice, Lochty.   *Owen Duffy*

Normal services eventually resumed but their future was by now uncertain and the final economic straw came when it became apparent that there was now an urgent need to relay the track on the entire length of the branch, it having had little money spent on its maintenance over many years and the permanent way was now in a poor state. The renewal costs were estimated at something in the region of £30,000, a sum which could not be justified by the present almost non-existent traffic or any possible flows in the future. Thus the Lochty branch, which had been born with such high hopes barely 70 years before, had reached its end - perhaps the most surprising fact being not that the line became a casualty of the Beeching era under a new Labour government* but that it had managed to survive two World Wars, the Grouping and nationalization with no real prospects of ever having to make even a minimal profit. Thus it was without ceremony that the last train operated on the branch on Saturday 8th August, 1964 and the line was closed to all traffic between Lochty and East Fife Central Junction with effect from Monday 10th August, 1964 along with the now unstaffed sidings at Kennoway, Montrave, Letham, Largoward and Lochty. A year later the Leven & East of Fife line between Leven and St Andrews via Elie, Anstruther and Crail was itself closed and the railway era in this part of Fife drew to an end.

The Lochty line was left to moulder for a couple of years while the weeds and vandals took over and then, in about 1967, the demolition contractors, Messrs T.W. Ward Ltd, began work. A BR class '24' diesel locomotive was used on the demolition trains and the removal of rails began at the eastern end of the line at Lochty, and continued back towards the junction near Leven. The track was cut into sections and placed by a crane on to wagons which were then taken to Ward's private siding at Inverkeithing while the sleepers were recovered by a caterpillar-type crawler tractor and stacked at the then railhead for onward transmission to local farmers for use as fencing, roads or firewood. The only other valuable material remaining was then the metal decking of the various underbridges on the line and these were cut up on site and winched on to lorries for removal while the trackbed of the railway was eventually sold to local landowners in a piecemeal fashion. Close to Letham a Leven-based firm of building contractors, Andrew Cook & Sons, purchased and then used the cutting there as a landfill site with the contents of their skips obliterating the route.

All in all the Lochty line was no more and over the years physical traces of it began to disappear from the landscape, maps and public memory but as a subsequent chapter reveals it was not the end of the railway at Lochty!

---

* It is shown in the goods map forming part of the Beeching report, *The Reshaping of British Railways*, as handling less than 5,000 tons of traffic per week but one suspects that in reality by this time that they barely handled 50 tons per week!

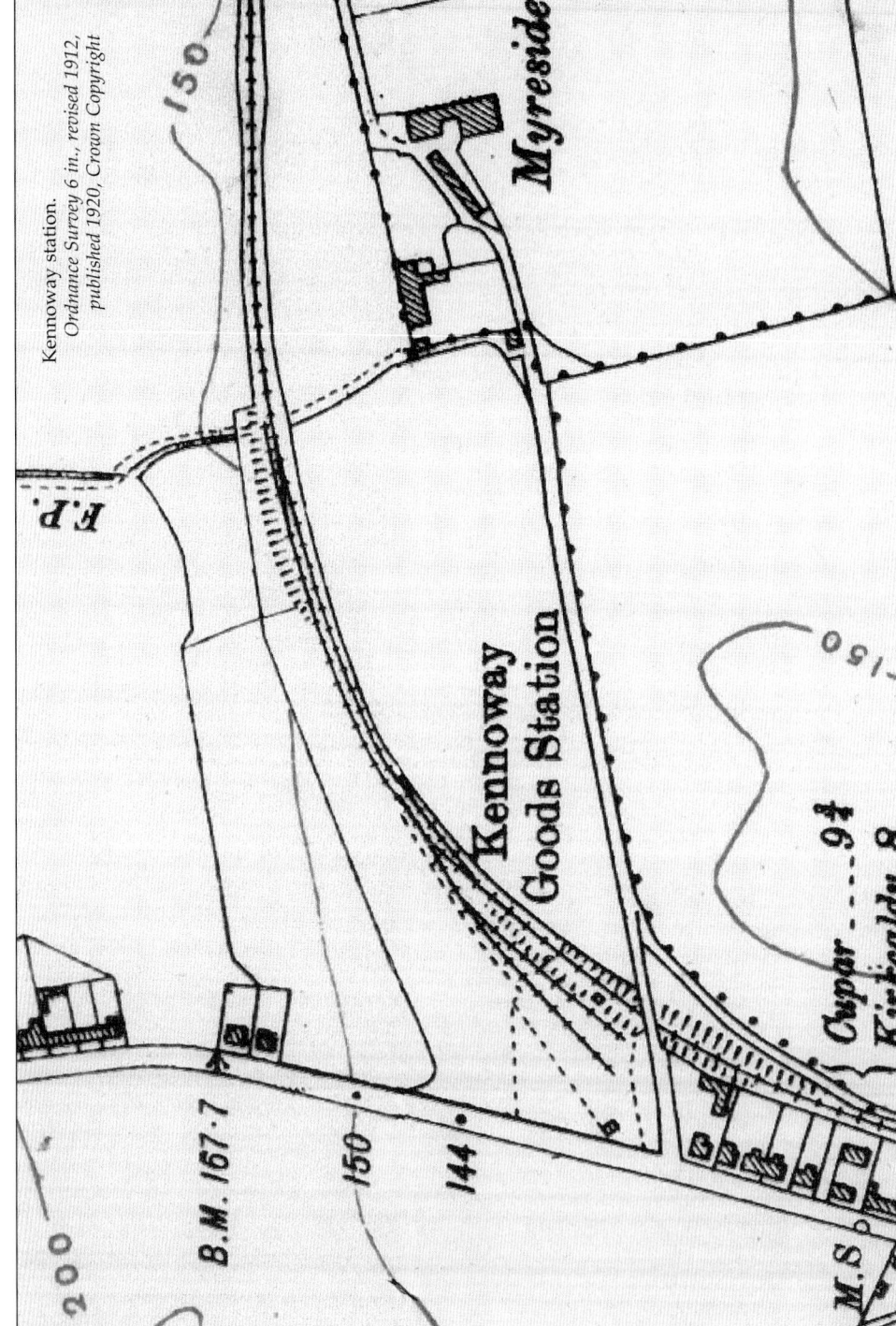

Kennoway station. Ordnance Survey 6 in., revised 1912, published 1920, Crown Copyright

Chapter Seven

A Picturesque Piece of Country: The East Fife Central Described

'The railway which is thus now part of the North British system
... traverses a very picturesque part of the country'
Leven Advertiser, 11th August, 1898

Some general observations

The following chapter describes the line in the heyday of its life in the years before World War I and although all of the features mentioned did not necessarily exist throughout the whole of the period of North British Railway ownership it should be assumed that the descriptions refer to 1914 unless otherwise indicated. The last Ordnance Survey one-inch map to show the line in its entirety was the Seventh Series one-inch map sheet 56 *St Andrews and Kirkcaldy* published in 1957. Road numbers follow the 1920 Ministry of Transport numbering scheme used for primary and secondary routes and in the Rigging generally correspond with the present numbers. Railway mileages are given in miles and chains (a chain equating to 22 yards or one-eightieth of a mile) and are given thus (0.00) from the junction with the Leven & East of Fife line.

The Lochty branch was single track throughout and worked from the outset as 'one engine in steam and No. 1 train staff' during daylight hours only. The designation 'down' side refers to the line running in the direction of Lochty while 'up' refers to the opposite direction. A nominal speed limit of 15 mph was in force throughout while whistle boards were erected at the level crossings at Balgrummo and Cairn. At the Burnside crossing all trains had to be brought to a complete halt while the fireman or guard had to open, and subsequently close, the gates there. The sidings at Kennoway, Letham, Montrave and Largoward were all worked by Annett's Key attached to the train staff; the working timetable note stated that this 'was for the purpose of preventing stray wagons from passing from them [the sidings] onto the main line'. There were no fixed signals other than those controlling the junction near Leven itself although telephone communication was maintained between all of the stations. The total length of the line was just over 14½ miles and the ruling gradient between the junction and Largoward was 1 in 70 rising and thereafter 1 in 70 falling to Lochty - according to the *Leven Advertiser* of 11th August, 1898 this made the line 'one of the steepest in Scotland'. The branch followed the coast line at a distance of roughly between one and four miles and climbing from just over sea level by the River Leven to reach of summit of 545 ft near to East Cassingray before falling back to 480 ft at the terminus.

East Fife Central Junction to Kennoway

The Lochty line left the Leven & East of Fife 'main' line just over half a mile to the west of Leven station at **East Fife Central Junction** (00.00) with a facing junction on the north side of the line protected by signals controlled from a brick-built signal box - this originally had a frame with 24 working levers (four spare and two spaces) and had a new frame installed in 1910 when the line between Leven and Thornton was

Alice passes underneath the Letham occupation bridge, 1898.   *John Howard*

Letham Farm Siding.   *Ordnance Survey 6 in., revised 1912, published 1920, Crown Copyright*

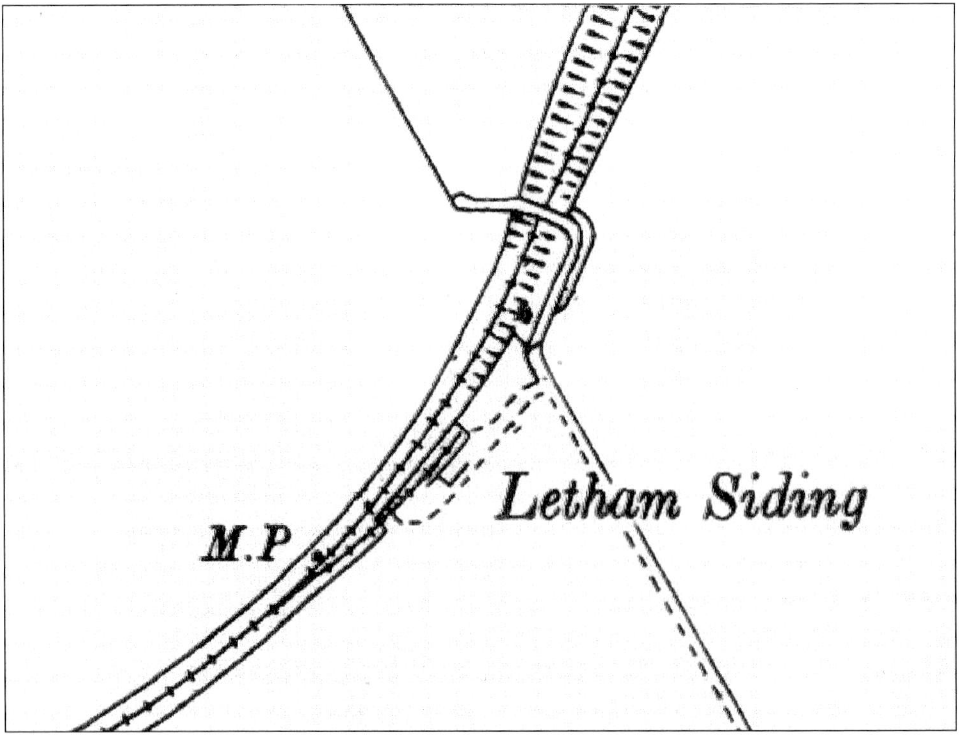

doubled; the box was closed on 3rd March, 1970. The branch line turned away from the River Leven in a north-facing sweeping arc before entering a cutting through a band of thick clay before passing under the Kirkcaldy to St Andrews road (A915) at Duniface below a typical stone-faced single-arch structure similar to those at Letham, Inverkellie and elsewhere on the line. By now climbing at the ruling gradient the line now ran parallel to the Windygates to Cupar road (A916), known locally as Sandy Brae, before entering **Kennoway Station**, (01.27), situated on the south side of the village which was then considerably smaller before the substantial building of houses there after the 1920s. The station here consisted of a short passenger platform on the down side together with a passing loop, loading bank and brick-built small goods office similar to those of the other stations on the line and two sidings from a trailing junction. The local gas works were situated next to the road on the down side and across the line lay a large metal gasholder which survived until the 1960s. On the up side of the line and to the east of the station was the Maiden Castle, an ancient conical earthwork with a medieval motte hill surmounting it - this was traditionally associated with Macduff, Thane of Fife.

Kennoway to Montrave

The line now turned to the north-east before passing under the Myreside bridge which carried a farm road over the line. The bridge had a steel-decked structure with stone and brick abutments similar to those seen (with minor variations) at many other places on the line such as Balgrummo, Baldutho and Teuchats Road and also on similar structures on the Aberlady line of the same contractor - several of these bridges still survive on both lines. Myreside farm was where the temporary buildings and sheds were temporarily erected for the building of the line. At Wester Durie the line passed over the Kennoway to Leven road and thereafter skirted the Durie estate before passing Balgrummo and the Burnside level crossing; here the small Back Burn was crossed. At Letham the line was crossed by a sturdy wooden occupation bridge which carried a farm track over the line - this structure, and a similar much-photographed bridge at Knightsward near Lochty, were both characteristic features of the line.* **Letham Farm Siding** (03.78), a single siding followed on a facing junction on the up side. The Leven to Montrave road (B927) now passed over the line on a substantial three-arched brick bridge while the unmistakable bulk of Largo Law dominated the skyline to the east. Within two miles **Montrave Station** (06.04) was reached, lying to the south of Greenside Farm. Similar in layout to Kennoway with its loading bank, goods office and station agent's house on the north of the down side, Montrave was situated in open countryside surrounded by the various farms which brought it business while Montrave House and its estate lay a short distance to the north and west.

---

* The structures were not unique and a similar occupation bridge was found at Milton on the Gifford & Garvald Light Railway - see the illustration on p.96 of *The Haddington, Macmerry and Gifford Branch Lines* (Oakwood Press,1994).

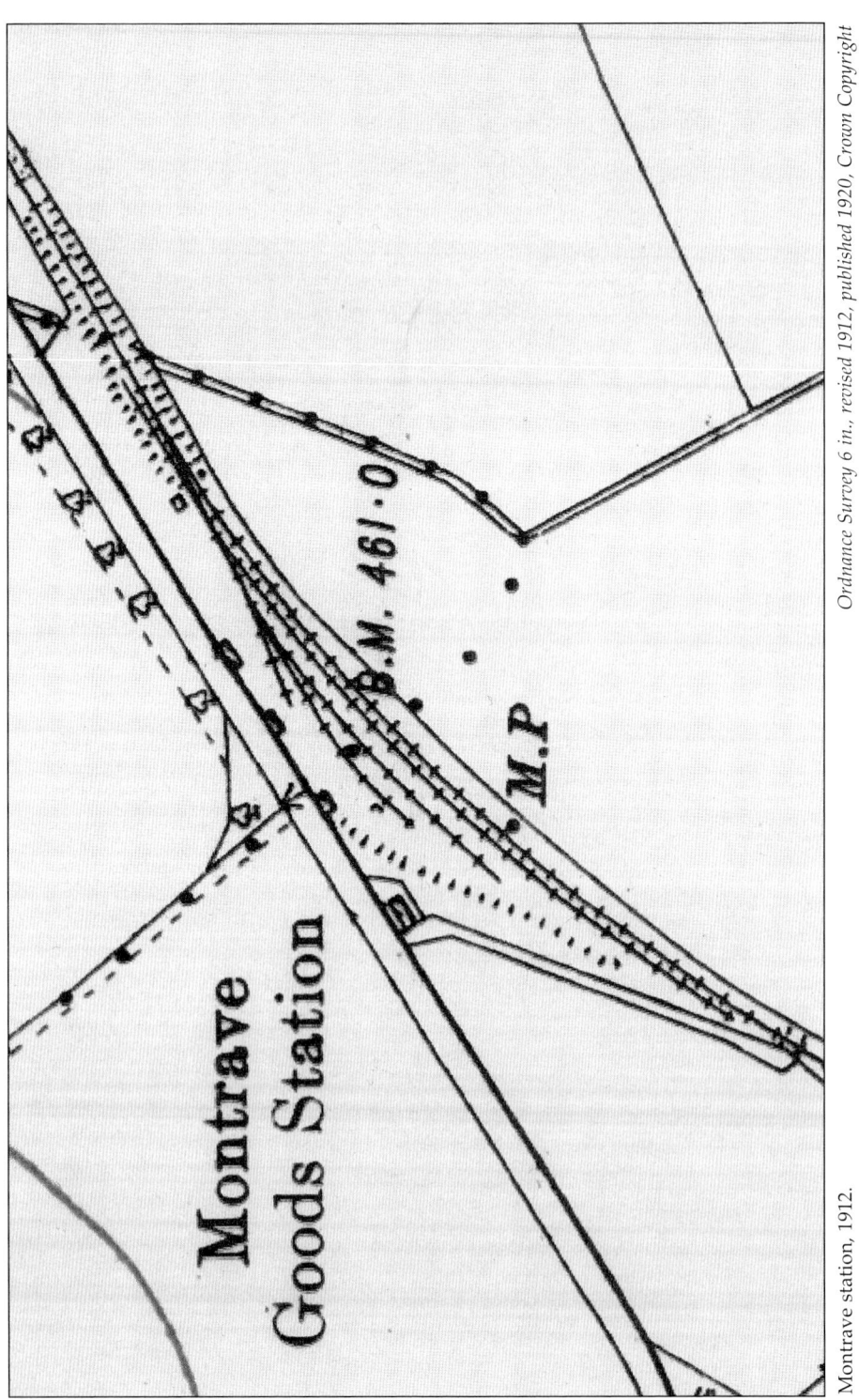

Montrave station, 1912.

Ordnance Survey 6 in., revised 1912, published 1920, Crown Copyright

The substantial wooden bridge at Bonnyton with the farm of that name in the background. *John Howard*

Montrave to Largoward

Beyond Montrave the site of the two proposed junctions at Teuchats on the northern line spurs that were never built are passed, before reaching Bonnyton where a substantial wooden bridge carried over the line over a lane leading to the farm of the same name which was close to the remains of an ancient earthwork, Norries Law. Then, beside the bridge carrying the lane from Baldastard farm to New Gilston over the line, was the former **Baldastard Colliery Siding** (07.55). This was an apparently single siding on the north side of the line with a facing junction; all traces had disappeared long before World War I. The line then bridged the Boghall Burn and the by-roads at East and West Gilston before cutting through a band of igneous rock and under the Largo to St Andrews main road (A915) before meeting a farm road at the Cairn level crossing and the lands of the Lathallan estate. **Largoward Station** (10.64) was then reached with the station agent's house and goods office to the north and the loading platform on the down side. Both buildings have survived and the goods office has been recently restored making this the best example of an extant railway structure on the whole line. Largoward was the busiest intermediate station on the East Fife Central, serving a wide hinterland of farms in the Rigging together with the village of Largoward itself, lying just to the north of the station and forming the largest settlement in the area.

Largoward in June 1952. *A.G. Ellis*

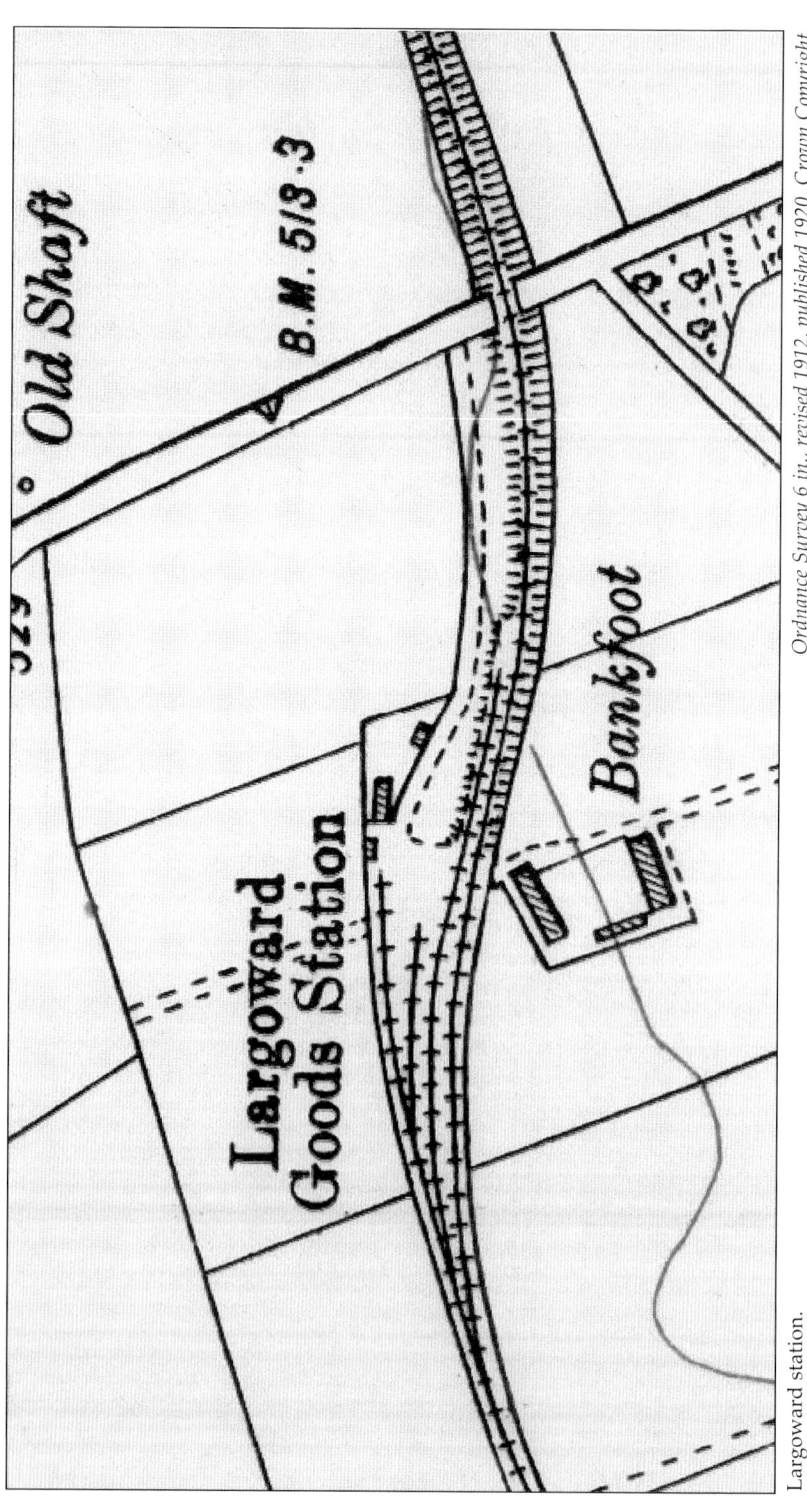

Largoward station. Ordnance Survey 6 in., revised 1912, published 1920, Crown Copyright

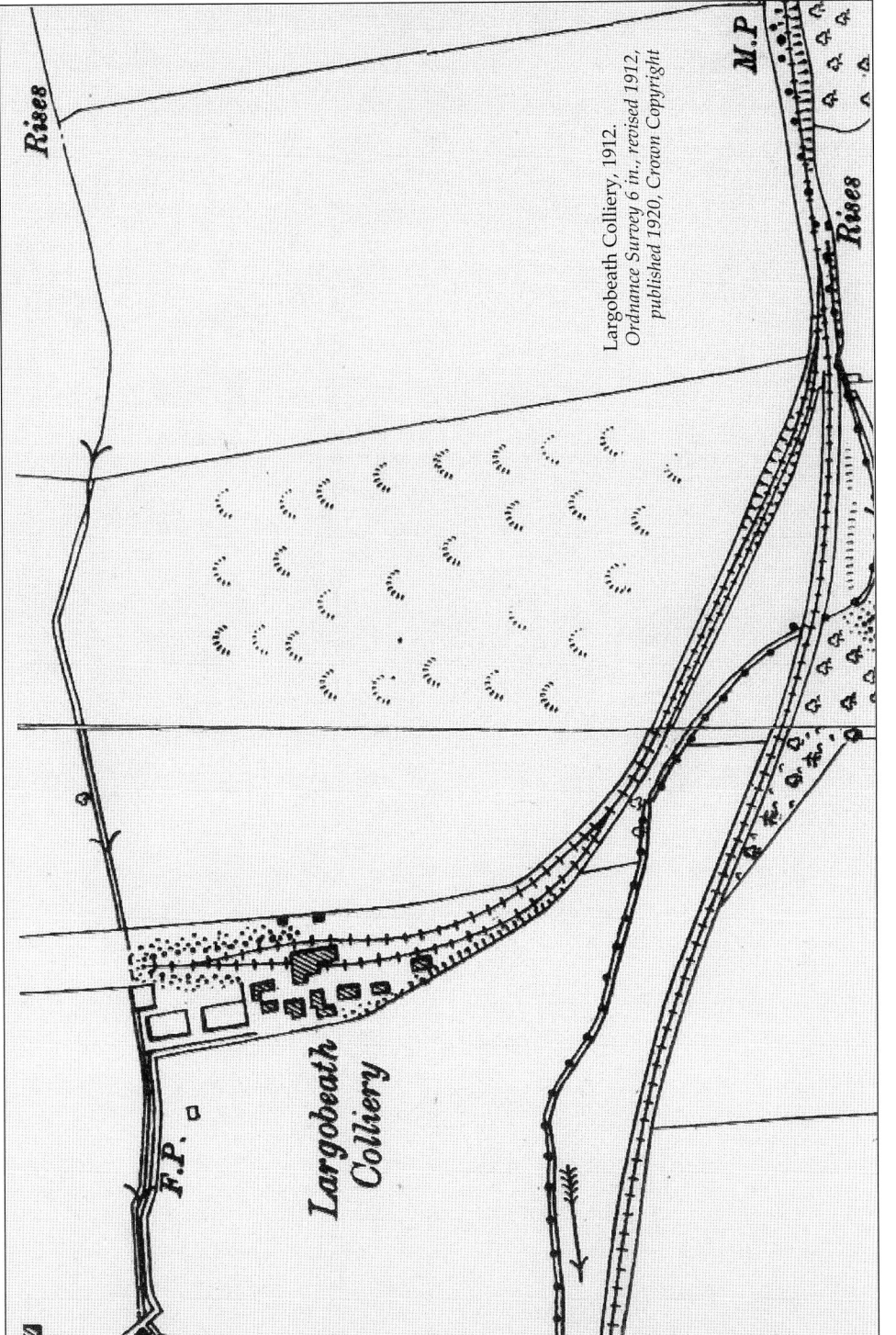

Largobeath Colliery, 1912. Ordnance Survey 6 in., revised 1912, published 1920, Crown Copyright

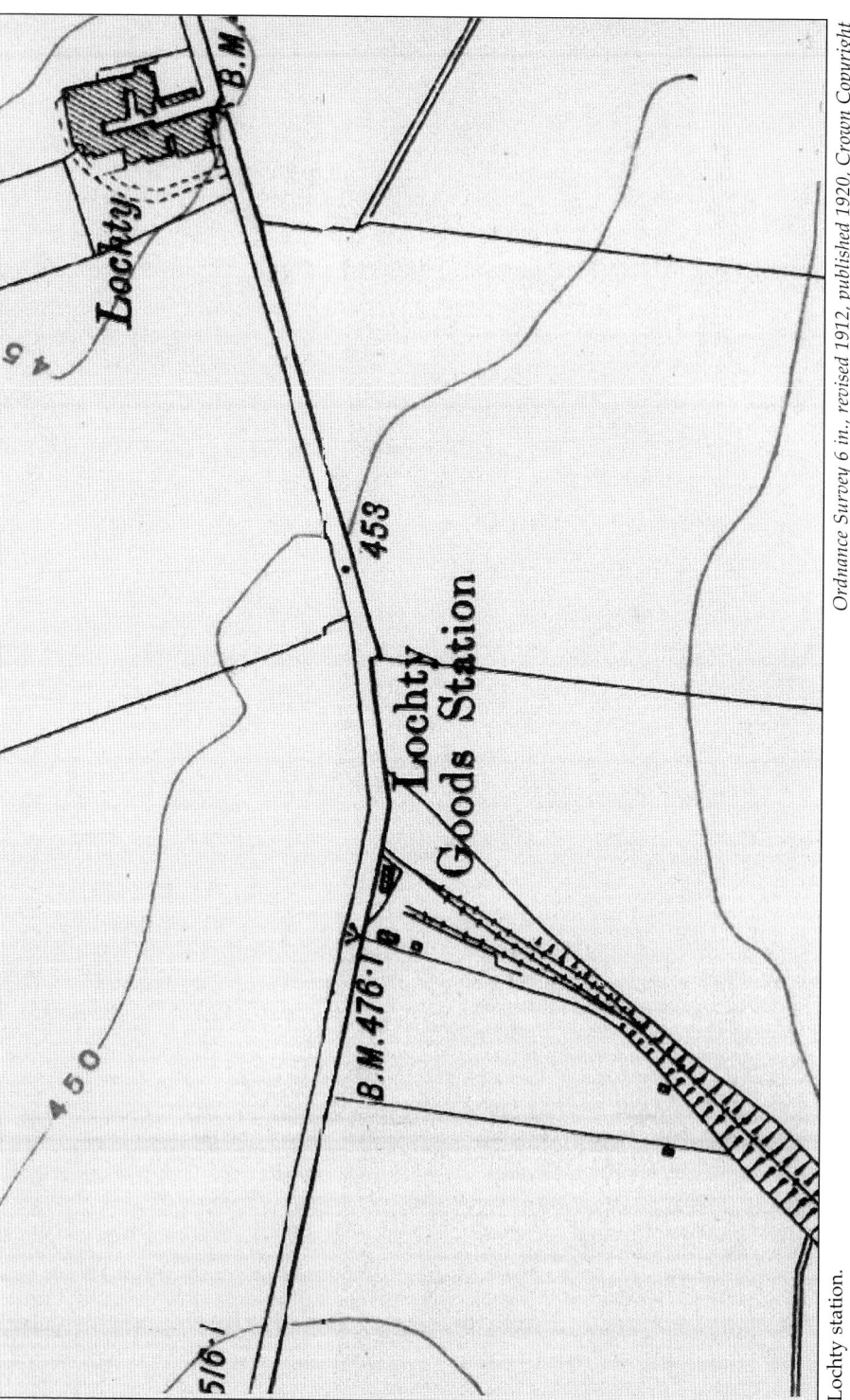

Lochty station.

Ordnance Survey 6 in., revised 1912, published 1920, Crown Copyright

Largoward to Lochty

The line now bridged the Kilconquhar to Peat Inn road (B941) and, passing through what was once the large Largoward coalfield reached the long-closed **Balcarres or Cassingray Colliery Siding** (11.52) on the north side of the line and then crossed the Den Burn. Then there followed, again on the up side, the **Largobeath Colliery Siding** (11.73), reached by a trailing junction and originally laid as a long double siding leading some 200 yards to the north-west of the branch and the passenger platform was situated on the up side of the line to the immediate west of the junction. Here the line had reached its summit and from then on dropped towards the terminus through a gentle rural aspect with the gentle Kellie Law rising up to the south along with the magnificent seaward view towards Pittenweem, the East Neuk coast, the Isle of May and the Firth of Forth together with the pleasing aspects of gently undulating and the distant views of the Isle of May. Crossing a feeder of the infant Dreel Burn at Baldutho the line now passed under the Arncroach to Knights Ward by-road at Over Kellie and passing by the site of the later halt of **Knightsward** (13.58), the later terminus situated on the down side of the Lochty Private Railway. A deep rock cutting was now entered, crossed by the wooden occupation bridge similar to that at Letham, before the line descended across open farmland to **Lochty Station** (14.50). Situated on the south side of the Crail to Cupar road (B940) a short distance to the west of the isolated Lochty Farm this is where the line terminated with a loading bank and goods office to the west of the sidings and the station agent's house to the north adjoining the road. It was a somewhat lonely and windswept location and although well suited to attract the sparse agricultural traffic of the surrounding but distant farms it was, on any view, a curious place in which to end a railway even by the somewhat optimistic but eccentric standards of the North British.

Overkellie bridge with *Mabel* arriving from the east. The identity of the marked individual is unknown. *John Howard*

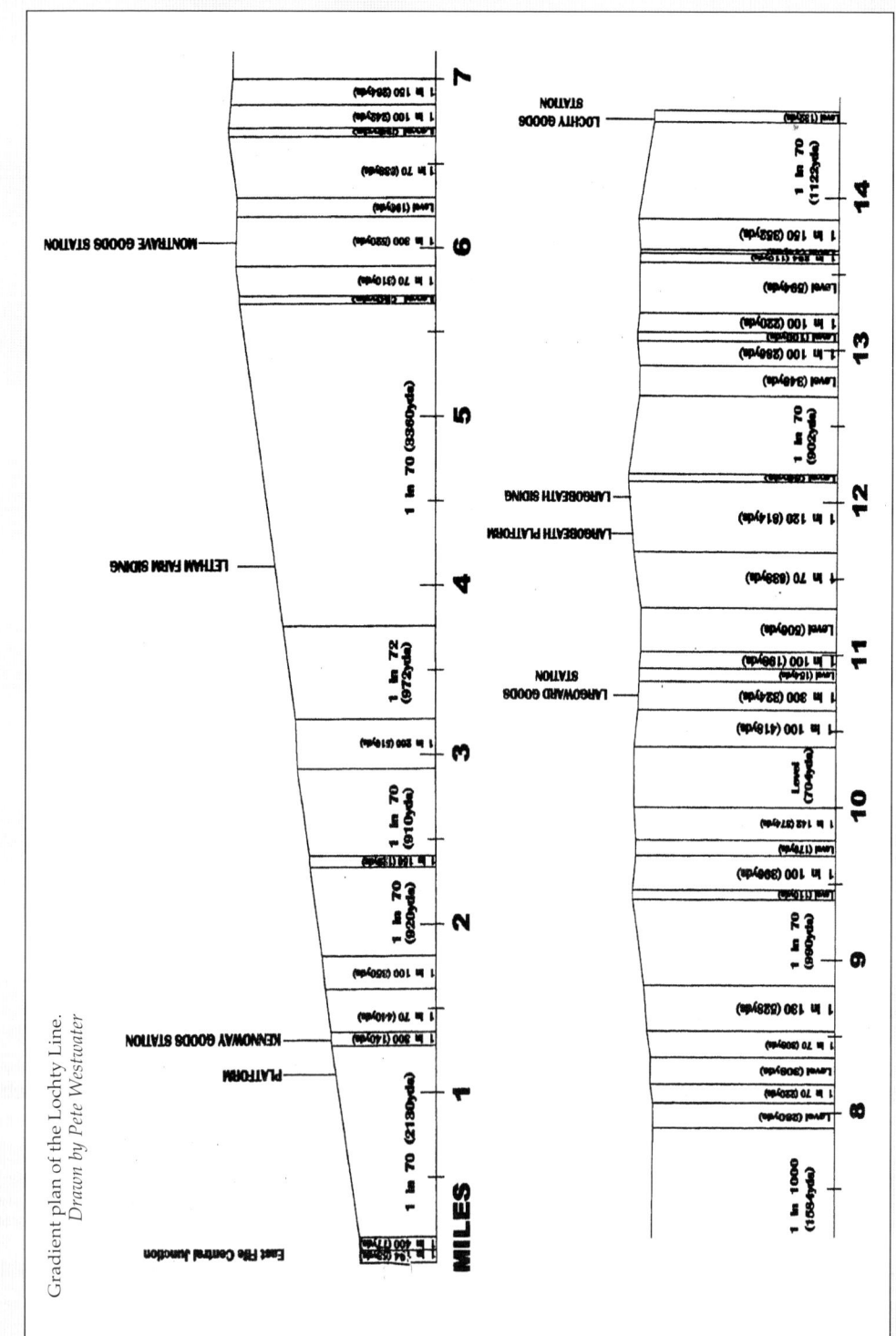

Gradient plan of the Lochty Line.
Drawn by Pete Westwater

Chapter Eight

Train Staffs and Traffic: Working the Lochty Branch

*'The mode of working is to be by train staff ...
no fixed signals or interlocking have been put in.'*
Leven Advertiser, 25th August, 1898

Stations and sidings

The public goods stations at Kennoway, Montrave, Largoward and Lochty were all originally staffed and connected to the North British by their own private telephone system. They had goods offices and stores, augmented by old carriages which ended their days as grounded sheds. Each station had a hand-operated crane of 2 ton capacity except Largoward which initially had a capacity of 1½ tons but was updated to deal with the same capacity as the other stations in 1938. All stations were held to be suitable for 'general goods traffic, furniture vans, carriages, motor cars, machines on wheels, livestock, parcels and miscellaneous traffic'. Resident staff were withdrawn from Kennoway in 1927 when it was placed under the supervision of Cameron Bridge station and from the other stations after World War II when Montrave, Largoward and Lochty were all placed under the control of the Kilconquhar station master. Eventually the stations become completely unstaffed and all orders for the collection or uplift of goods had to be placed by telephone with the goods clerks at Cameron Bridge, Kilconquhar or Anstruther. The station agents' houses still remained in the occupation of railway employees or retired employees although they generally deteriorated in condition and no proper attempts were made to upgrade the domestic facilities there. The sidings at Letham were under the supervision of Montrave and thereafter Kilconquar and Balcarres, Baldastard and Largobeath under the control of Largoward. Kennoway station also handled coal traffic for the adjacent gas works and also had a domestic coal depot owned by the Fife Coal Co. The remaining siding at Letham was latterly under the control of Anstruther.

Traffic

The figures for each station on the branch and covering the period between 1900 and 1934 are given in *Appendix Two* of this book. The agricultural traffic dealt with at all stations was basically similar and inward traffic consisted of cattle feed (including local distillery draff, a by-product of whisky manufacturing), fertiliser (which included Belgian furnace slag containing ammonia, inorganic fertilisers and manure-based products), lime, livestock purchased at market, seed and miscellaneous farm supplies while outward traffic consisted of seed potato traffic bound for the South, sugar beet bound for Cupar, cattle and (principally from Montrave) sheep for English markets especially London and, in early years, there was a good traffic in horses but there was no substantial rail traffic in pigs. Coal traffic consisted of inward traffic principally from Fife pits and outward traffic from Balcarres and Largobeath and, to a smaller extent, from the small local workings such as Kilmux* and Radernie. As the use of motor vehicles became common from

---

* See an article by W. Reid in the *East Fife Mail* of 11th July, 1979.

The entrance to Kennoway station, July 1953. Note the removal of the LNER cast letters.
J.L. Stevenson

The entrance to Lochty station, July 1953. *J.L. Stevenson*

Gilson bridge after closure, 1964. *Owen Duffy*

Unloading fertilisers at Largoward, June 1952. *J.L. Stevenson*

Shunting in progress at Largoward, January 1964. *Owen Duffy*

Dropping three wagons off at Montrave before proceeding on to Lochty, 25th March, 1961.
M.B. Smith

The goods office at Largoward in 1963. This pleasing little NBR structure has been restored as a residence and survives to this day. *Owen Duffy*

the 1920s onwards rail traffic began to decline particularly in respect of livestock and, from 1947 onwards, unfavourable pricing by BR combined with a declining use of coal for domestic and agricultural purposes made rail traffic even less attractive. One interesting development was that although all of the stations and sidings were still open, albeit latterly on an unstaffed basis, traffic seemed to have been concentrated at Largoward. After closure of the line in 1964 such traffic that had not already been lost to road competition was transferred to Leven Dock (Shorehead) siding (replacing Kennoway), Lundin Links (for Montrave traffic), Anstruther and Cupar (for Largoward traffic) and Pittenweem (for Lochty), but within a few years all of the goods traffic had succumbed to the lorry.

Services

From the opening of the line a daily service was provided to all stations and sidings to Lochty with a morning departure and afternoon return and this appears to have been adequate to cope with all traffic with only a few additional trains run in early years largely as a result of inadequate motive power. An additional trip working, run 'as required' but probably on a near-daily basis and by the Leven pilot engine, was a coal working from Kirkland Yard to Kennoway to serve the gas works at the latter location. The Largobeath colliers trains were operated separately from the goods services. From the cessation of the Largobeath coal traffic the daily goods service was reduced to a thrice-weekly service to Largoward with a single train continuing on to Lochty. In May 1918 the service was:

		A	B			B	A
East Fife Central Jn	dep.	11.25	11.25	Lochty	dep.	___	1.15
Kennoway	dep.	11.40	11.40	Largoward	dep.	1.05	1.40
Montrave	dep.	12.05	12.05	Montrave	dep.	1.35	2.15
Largoward	dep.	12.40	12a 5	Kennoway	dep.	2.05	2.45
Lochty	arr.	12.55		East Fife Central Jn	arr.	2.15	2.55

A - Does not run on Tuesdays and Thursdays B - Tuesdays and Thursdays only
a arrive

At the end of World War I a service of all three weekly trains travelling all the way to Lochty was again instituted and this pattern of trains on Tuesdays, Thursdays and Saturdays only was maintained throughout World War II and right up to closure of the line in 1964; the same timings applied throughout the whole of the 45 year period although the trains running beyond Largoward sometimes consisted of only the engine and a single brake van.

The branch workings were latterly dealt with as a trip working from Thornton and in 1960 'working B114, hauled by a Class 3F (J36) engine' was operated as follows:

	arr.	dep.	
	am	am	
Thornton		8.25	(light engine)
Thornton Yard	8.35	8.50	
Cameron Bridge		9.25	(calls if required)
Leven	9.58	10.15	
Lundin Links	10.22	10.30	

'J36' No. 65345 approaching Burnside, 18th February, 1961. *W.S. Sellar*

Mud on the snowplough of No. 65345 at Methil East signal box, 18th February, 1961. *W.S. Sellar*

	arr.	dep.	
	am	am	
Leven	10.37	10.50	
Cameron Bridge	10.58	11.20	
Leven	11.30	11.50	
	pm	pm	
Lochty	1.50	2.05	
Kirkland Yard	3.45	3.55	
Cameron Bridge		4.10	
Thornton Yard	4.45	4.45	(light engine)
Thornton Engine Shed	4.55		

Owing both to the absence of signalling and adequate lighting and the general need only to operate a single train service there was no necessity ever to use the line outwith daylight hours.

Locomotive power

The first locomotive to work on the Lochty line was apparently an elderly Hurst 0-6-0 No. 190 dating from 1861 and this 'third class engine', which was so described by William Arnott in the letter quoted on page 36, was roundly criticized as being underpowered for the uphill gradients on the branch. On one occasion No. 190 operated the 11.20 am Leven to Lochty service and its 1.15 return working with seven loaded and four empty wagons on the outward run and 16 loaded and 15 empty from Lochty back to Leven and this was regarded as unremarkable.* By the turn of the century the Hurst locomotives had been replaced by one of the NBR Holmes class 'C' 5 ft (LNER 'J36') goods 0-6-0 locomotives and these sturdy engines, built in the late Victorian era, were thought to be ideal for branch line use and they formed the largest class of locomotive on the NBR. For years these versatile engines formed the mainstay of the Lochty service and were also seen at work throughout Fife for more than 60 years from the opening of the East Fife Central. The LNER official Route Availability for the line was classed as '4', permitting an axle loading of approximately 17½ tons, and over the years additional types of locomotive appeared including the larger and more modern NBR Reid 5 ft class 'B' ('J35') 0-6-0s (which had an axle loading of 18 tons) and the 'N15' Reid class 'A' 0-6-2T locomotives destined for Leven Dock and Methil services. In latter years 'J36' class 0-6-0 No. 65345 was a stalwart on the line - this locomotive, built at Cowlairs in 1900, out-lived the Lochty branch and when withdrawn in 1966 along with sister locomotive No. 65288 had the distinction of being the last two steam locomotives in service on the Scottish Region of British Railways - despite this honour both were sold as scrap to Arnott Young of Carmyle, Glasgow. The larger 'J35' 0-6-0s including Nos. 64474, 64478, 64522 and 64488 were also seen on the Lochty branch on various occasions until the last 'J35s' were withdrawn in 1962. In view of the preponderance of mud on the line brought by tractors on the various occupation crossings locomotives were often fitted with small snowploughs, it was said to assist with the clearing of this debris, although how successful this was compared to their undoubtedly efficient and much needed snow clearing activities is doubtful. An additional class of locomotive, the BR Standard '4MT' 2-6-4Ts was also allowed from 1962.†

* BR/NBR/4/430, *Statement Showing Goods Trains Working on Thursday 20th October 1898*, a unique NBR record of goods services being operated on what was regarded as a normal day - no comments appear to suggest that the Lochty service was exceptional on that date.
† BR (Sc) Supplementary Instructions, 18th June, 1962.

The first locomotive to operate the East Fife Central Railway. NBR Hurst 0-6-0 No. 190 seen at Anstruther with driver George Pitblado at the turn of the century.

NBRSG Hennigan Collection

'J35' class 0-6-0 No. 64478 with a tender cab at Largoward on the Lochty railtour, 20th January, 1962.

J.L. Stevenson Collection

TRAIN STAFFS AND TRAFFIC 79

Hunslet 0-6-0DM D2584 at Largoward, July 1963. *Owen Duffy*

The station buildings at Lochty with Hunslet No. D2583 at rest, April 1963. *Owen Duffy*

Above: BR Standard class '4' 4-6-0 No. 76111 on the Lochty branch with the breakdown train, January 1963. *Below:* A NBR seven-compartment third built in 1902-05 and in use on the breakdown train near Lathallan, 1963. *(Both) Neil Woods*

An old NBR four-wheel third of 1870-72 vintage in use as a shed at Lochty in the 1960s.
Owen Duffy

The crew standing beside Hunslet No. D2585 at Lochty, April 1963. *Owen Duffy*

One important point to be considered was that there were no water columns or tanks for engine water supply on the line, the nearest water column being at Cameron Bridge station and the absence of any water supply meant that any locomotive type used on the line needed to carry its own water; thus only tender locomotives or large tank engines would suffice.

In 1962 three of the small Methil-based 0-6-0 204 hp diesel shunters built by the Hunslet Engine Co. of Leeds, Nos. D2583, D2584 and D2585, began to operate services along with the 'J36s' and it is thought that one of these diesels in fact operated the last ever normal goods service on the line in 1964. Motive power on the Lochty line was in all instances based at Thornton shed.

Signals, crossings and speed restrictions

There were no signal boxes or fixed signals on the Lochty line beyond East Fife Central Junction and the line was operated on the 'one engine in steam (No. 1 train staff)' principle. The sidings at Kennoway, Letham, Montrave and Largoward were all worked by Annett's Key attached to the train staff. A speed limit of 15 mph was in operation over the whole line. The public and occupation level crossings on the line were all ungated except for that at Burnside (near to Letham) where the following notice applied:

> All trains and engines working over this branch must be brought to a complete stand before reaching the level crossing, and, in the case of up trains the fireman will open the gates and close and re-lock them after the train or engine has passed, while in the case of down trains, that duty will be performed by the guard or (where there is no guard) the fireman.

Whistle boards were erected at the open level crossings at Balgrummo and Cairn where it was thought that they were needed because of the limited vision there, although the sound of a whistle did not prevent an accident at the latter in 1961. Other local hazards included lineside fires when vegetation was prone to catch fire in dry weather - the section of line between Kennoway and Montrave was particularly vulnerable.*

---

* *BR Supplementary Operating Instructions (SE), 29 April 1957 until further notice.* The risks of lineside fires were said to be greatest between January and May between 5 miles 1,088 yards and 5 miles, 1,320 yards.

No. 65345 on the Lochty branch goods at East Fife Central Junction, 18th February, 1961.
W.S. Sellar

The interior of the junction signal box. *Owen Duffy*

Chapter Nine

Phoenix on the Farm:
The Lochty Private Railway 1967-1992

*'Thus was born what at the time was Britain's
shortest standard gauge preserved railway'*
Steven Dewar, Fife Railway Preservation Group, 1991

A new home for No. 9

The demolition of the Lochty branch was not, however, the end of the story for the former East Fife Central line for part of it was to have the dubious distinction of being both the first preserved railway to open in Scotland and the first to close. The story began in August 1966 when farmer Mr John B. Cameron* bought Lochty Farm, including the site of the former goods terminal (the buildings having been demolished) and the solum of the trackbed of the final section of the abandoned branch line. He was a lifelong railway enthusiast and great admirer of steam engines in general and in particular the 'A4' Pacific locomotives of the LNER. These locomotives, designed by Edinburgh-born Sir Nigel Gresley and built at Doncaster between 1935 and 1938, achieved an instant success as the racehorses of the East Coast main line and of the 35 built the most famous of them all, the renowned *Mallard*, in 1938 achieved and still holds the world speed record (126 mph) for steam locomotives. No. 9, later BR No. 60009, *Union of South Africa*,† had an illustrious career including being a designated Royal engine in the 1950s and was in 1963 the last ever steam engine to be overhauled at the works in which she was built. The following year she worked the last 'A4'-hauled train out of Kings Cross and was then sent to Ferryhill depot in Aberdeen to enjoy her swansong hauling the smartly-timed new three-hour express services between Glasgow and Aberdeen.

Withdrawn in the summer of 1966 as part of the general final run-down of steam in Scotland, No. 9 evaded the scrapyard by being purchased for about £3,000 (her scrap value) by John Cameron, although its tender was found to be defective and the locomotive was coupled with the tender of another withdrawn member of the class, No. 60004 *William Whitelaw*. After transfer to Thornton and held there for the winter No. 9 reappeared for the special farewell to steam in Scotland excursion on 26th March, 1967 and then No. 9 and her new tender made their way on 8th April, 1967 behind an English Electric class '08' diesel shunter from Thornton to Crail, forming the last freight item over the Leven & East of Fife line# and by then taken separately by road by a team of Pickford's Scammell tractors and low loaders to Lochty.

* John Cameron CBE, to whom the authors are grateful for his assistance with researching this book, still retains interests in farming but no longer owns Lochty Farm. He was the Chairman of ScotRail and a member of the British Railways Board and subsequently was a Director of Stagecoach, South West Trains and the Isle of Wight Island Line and was a member of the Safety Review Group and is the President of the Gresley Society. He is now the owner of LNER 'K4' class 2-6-0 No. 3442 *The Great Marquess* as well as No. 9 and now lives at Balbuthie, St Monans.
† Originally to be called *Osprey* the locomotive was re-named after the Dominion predecessor of the *Republic of South Africa* before entering service; it reverted to its intended name for a short period in the 1990s when that country became politically temporarily unpopular.
# Further details and pictures of this journey are given in the present authors' *Leven & East of Fife Railway*, Oakwood Press, 2013.

No. 9 coming out of its small shed at Lochty with Dave Murray standing on the right.
P.M. Westwater

John Cameron driving his own engine at Lochty in 1967.
P.M. Westwater

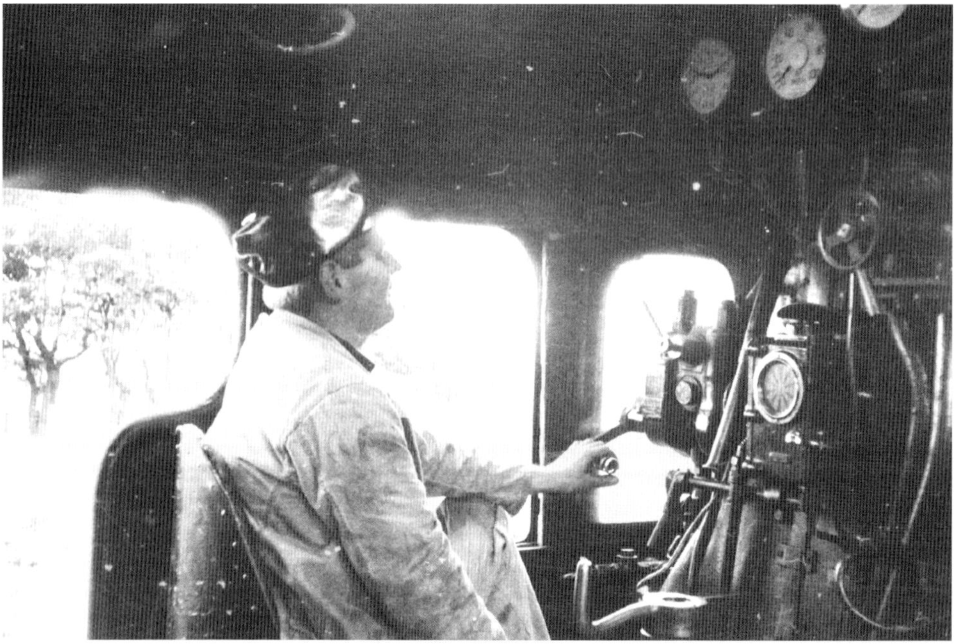

No. '9 STEAMS AGAIN!

VISIT LOCHTY PRIVATE RAILWAY COMPANY AND SEE SCOTLAND'S ONLY REMAINING PACIFIC LOCOMOTIVE IN STEAM.

Opening Day — SUNDAY, 18th JUNE

GATES OPEN 2 p.m.

See Ex-L.N.E.R. Streamlined Class A.4, No. 60009 "UNION OF SOUTH AFRICA" in full working order.

Britain's Most Famous Type of Locomotive.

SUNDAY AFTERNOONS from 18th JUNE till MID-SEPTEMBER

Half-Hourly Departures from 3 p.m. till 6.30 p.m.

LOCHTY STATION 5 MILES FROM ANSTRUTHER

ADMISSION 5/-   CHILDREN (under 14) 2/6   CAR PARK FREE

Printed by J. & G. Innes Ltd., Burnside, Cupar

'No. 9 Steams Again!'. The first ever handbill issued by the Lochty Private Railway in 1967.
P.M. Westwater

The diminutive halt at Knightsward.   J.L. Stevenson

The engine shed at Lochty, 16th June, 1967.   J.L. Stevenson

The railway returns

John Cameron, determined to see trains running again in this by-now remote from the railway part of the East Neuk and wanting something to run No. 9 on, acquired second-hand track from the National Coal Board's recently closed Glencraig Colliery in West Fife. He laid the track on the last ¾ mile of the branch line to form a private line on which to operate No. 9 through his land. John Cameron, his wife and some friends formed the Lochty Railway Co., later renamed the Lochty Private Railway (LPR).

On 14th June, 1967, before an invited audience of over 200 guests, Gordon Stewart, Assistant General Manager, British Rail (ScR), unveiled a plaque on the driver's cab side to commemorate the first run by this engine on what was now known as the Lochty Private Railway. With No. 9 as the prime attraction, a large number of visitors arrived at Lochty to view the locomotive and enjoy a footplate journey in the summer and autumn of 1967 and as a result a carriage was purchased to accommodate the expected visitors for the next season. This carriage, LNER 'Coronation' observation car No. E1719 (the beaver-tail coach had been modified in 1965 to work on the West Highland line), was purchased and this resulted in a total of 3,000 passengers being conveyed in 1968, the year in which the last BR steam engines ran in normal service.

In the winter of 1970 the line was extended a further ¼ mile to Knightsward using track recovered from the recently closed St Andrews branch line so that it was possible to run a two-mile there and back trip behind No. 9 and a diminutive platform named 'Knightsward' after the adjacent farm of that name was built on the north side of the line. A further coach, this time a BR Mark I carriage (BSO No. E9513 built at Doncaster in 1965), was purchased to enable passengers to travel on a two-coach train. This coach was transferred by rail from Glasgow to Kirkland Yard and from there hauled by a diesel shunter to Lawson's coal yard at Leven Dock Siding and from there by road where 'a few of the people who assisted with its loading sat in the coach on its way to Lochty, much to the amazement of several shoppers in Largo'.*

A working steam railway

From early days a number of local enthusiasts, originally from the Glenrothes Model Railway Club and later from elsewhere in Fife, turned up to assist John Cameron with the maintenance of the Lochty Private Railway, No. 9 and the observation car. In due course the enthusiasts formed the operating staff on the line and at the terminus at Lochty. The success of the railway in attracting visitors was almost immediate - in 1968 almost 3,000 visitors turned up while in the following years the totals were about 5,000 and then 7,000.† In April 1973, after the policy of running steam engines again on BR lines had been reversed, No. 9 was returned to the main line and it was then intended to turn the LPR into a working steam museum and those volunteers who made up the workforce on the LPR formed the Fife Railway Preservation Group (FRPG). In due course the trackwork was renewed and a number of smaller locomotives were acquired starting with Bagnall Austerity

* Steven Dewar.
† The 1970 comparative figure for the Festiniog Railway was 352,000 but the scale of the operations on both lines was hardly similar!

No. 9 on a train at the occupation bridge, 1972. *P.M. Westwater*

No. 9 at the end of the line, Knightsward, 1971. *P.M. Westwater*

0-6-0 saddle tank of 1944 vintage which had formerly been on the the MOD at Kineton and latterly became Wemyss Private Railway No. 16 in 1965. No. 16 had latterly been standing in Thomas Muir's scrapyard at Wester Balbeggie near Thornton and after being purchased arrived at Lochty on 7th April, 1973 on the same transporter that had removed No. 9 to BR metals at Ladybank a few days earlier. No. 16 was later joined by three 0-4-0 saddle tanks, namely Peckett Works No. 1376 of 1915 which had formerly been Burntisland Aluminium Co. No. 1, Scottish Gas Board No. 10 (Barclay Works No. 1890 of 1926) which was from the Edinburgh Corporation's Granton Gas Works and National Coal Board 21 (Barclay Works No. 2292 of 1951) which was the last steam locomotive to work at Frances Colliery in Dysart. These engines were owned by or lent to the FRPG and were also operated along with five other diesel locomotives:

NCB No. 10 (North British Loco. Co. 0-6-0 27591 of 1957)
LPR No. 4 (Ruston Works No. 421415 of 1958)
LPR No. 34 (Ruston 0-4-0 diesel-hydraulic Works No. 506399 of 1964)
RAF 400 (North British Loco. Co. Works No. 27421 of 1957)
RAF 405 (North British Loco. Co. Works No. 27426)

The two RAF locomotives had previously operated on the aerodrome line at Leuchars and were named respectively *River Eden* and *River Tay*. In addition two further Mk I carriages (TSO SC4223 of 1956 and SC14010 a BFK of 1960) were acquired from a stockpile at Millerhill Yard near Edinburgh and delivered via the sidings of John Haig & Co. at Markinch. In addition 14 wagons had been acquired from a number of sources and attempts were made to preserve some of them in local Fife liveries. In addition a brake van, rail crane and other equipment was obtained and some lattice post signals, two of which were from the Michael Colliery, were erected, a shed and small wooden building serving as a souvenir shop and ticket office were built.

Day return to Knightsward

The basic passenger service, which was operated on Sunday afternoons through the season which normally ran from early June to the beginning of September, ran at frequent intervals from Lochty to Knightsward with a running time of 7-8 minutes each way with a five minute wait at the western end of the line. Normally there were no public services outside of this period. Tickets were issued and the 1970 return fare was 4s. 0d. Mention was made in a timetable of a request halt at Lochty Dyke being only served by certain trains travelling towards Lochty but this was not a formal stop but a point which was recognized by the volunteer staff as an unofficial point lying beside the wooden occupation bridge.

The Lochty Private Railway was open to the public as a 'heritage' line and was maintained chiefly by volunteers, initially mainly from the Glenrothes Model Railway Club but, from 1974 onwards, also from the Fife Railway Preservation Group. No. 9 operated the service until it returned to the former BR parcels shed at Kirkcaldy before being moved to the main line at Markinch in October from where it was readily available to haul enthusiasts' specials on the main line. The replacement motive power on the Lochty line was now supplied by two small industrial tank engines with a good Fife provenance and acquired by John Cameron

THE EAST FIFE CENTRAL RAILWAY

Adult (blue) and child (pink) tickets on the LPR, 1970.

Lochty Private Railway 1973 timetable. Note the mention of the request halt at 'Lochty Dyke' although there was no permanent platform there.

LOCHTY PRIVATE RAILWAY

	Sundays 10 June to 2 September inclusive								
Lochty .... dep	14.00	14.30	15.00	15.30	15.50	16.10	16.30	17.00
Knightsward .... arr	14.07	14.37	15.07	15.37	15.57	16.17	16.37	17.07
		sd		sd		sd		
Knightsward ....dep	14.12	14.42	15.12	15.40	16.00	16.20	16.42	17-12
Lochty .... arr	14.20	14.50	15.20	15.48	16.08	16.28	16.50	17.20

sd Stops at Lochty Dyke to set down only
Guard to be informed before leaving Knightsward

Inside the observation car, 29th July, 1973. *John H. Meredith*

PHOENIX ON THE FARM

No. 16 at Thomas Muir's scrapyard near Thornton in the process of being rescued, 1973.
P.M. Westwater

No. 16 on a Foden low loader emerging from the scrapyard at Easter Balbeggie Farm on its way for a new life at Lochty, 7th April, 1973.
P.M. Westwater

No. 16 with a train of the LNER observation car and a BR Mark I near Knightsward.
P.M. Westwater

No. 9 leaving Lochty for the last time, 1973.
P.M. Westwater

'Neccesity being the mother of invention' - using the bridge to lift the saddle tank of No. 16 the hard way.
P.M. Westwater

The Peckett with a single carriage train at the occupation bridge.
P.M. Westwater

A reprieved BR Mark I passing through Leven on its way to Lochty on the back of a Pickford Scammel trailer in 1974. *P.M. Westwater*

Ruston-hauled goods with vintage restored Fife wagons including Wemyss Coal Company and Tullis Russell examples. *P.M. Westwater*

An open wagon restored to the livery of one of the Fife coalmasters. P.M. Westwater

NBR box van restored at Lochty, 1970. Mike Jodeluk

from Muir's scrapyard. In 1973 the advertised service consisted of a train leaving Lochty on the hour and half-hour between 14.00 and 17.00 with a return journey leaving Knightsward at 12 and 42 minutes past the hour from 14.12 until 17.12. The journey time in the outward direction was seven minutes with eight being allowed for the return. Given the absence of a turntable trains made the return journey with the locomotive propelling the train; water was taken at Lochty. Headboards were often carried with the somewhat inappropriate titles such as the 'Bon Accord' or 'Fife Coast Express'! Given that the line did not enter public property it was operated on a deliberately friendly and informal basis and passengers were welcomed on to the footplate when the engine was stationary. The line was deliberately run by a small number of dedicated and enthusiastic members who were all expected to contribute to running the line with their manpower. Given that some 18 members ran eight return services on some 13 Sundays every summer for many years the Lochty Private Railway was a somewhat unique line, far removed from the more famous and 'professional' preserved railways in other parts of Britain but nevertheless was a much-loved and keenly-anticipated part of any holiday in the East Neuk.

The drivers of No. 9 in its Lochty days were all BR-qualified steam locomotive drivers, namely Tommy Farrell (a BR driver), Jock Buchanan (chief locomotive inspector for BR Scottish Region) and John Cameron. After No. 9 left Lochty and No. 16 was the leading steam locomotive the drivers were Tommy Farrell and Jimmy Hogg, another BR-trained driver. The firemen of the Lochty steam locomotives were not professional railwaymen but dedicated amateurs and included Ian Leven and the late Davy Murray.The greatest traffic ever carried on the LPR was on Saturday 5th June, 1976 when No. 16 did 10 round trips to Knightsward and carried 1,500 cub scouts in total - they were having their Jubilee camp in a field at Lochty and this was also the only day on which the line operated a Saturday as opposed to Sunday service!

The Guide to the LPR contained the following warning to those visiting the line:

> If you would like to take photographs around Lochty or Knightsward stations you can only do so upon the purchase of a lineside permit., which can be bought at the ticket office or the shop when the ticket office is closed. Once on or about the yards do look out for trains as we cannot take account for every necessary movement of our rolling stock also you may be obscured behind a building or an item of rolling stock. Most importantly do not at any time walk or stray onto or about the running lines as you may be putting yourself or others in danger. REMEMBER TRAINS MOVE ANY TIME, ANY PLACE, ANYWHERE!

A second closure

After a quarter of a century of Sunday train services, sharp increases in public liability insurance premiums (the cover of which had risen from £500,000 in 1967 to £2million in 2002) and the realization that holidaymakers now apparently required more sophisticated facilities such as toilets and refreshment facilities and that a mile-long line in an isolated rural setting could not raise the financial resources to fund these, the Lochty Private Railway's shareholders took the decision in September 1992 to cease running the line at the close of the season. Lochty lost its trains for the second and final time. The track was lifted in the autumn of the year by FRPG members. Starting at Knightsward the track was lifted using the rail crane owned by the Group and was cut into sections before being placed on flat wagons and taken to Lochty for T. Muir Ltd, a Kirkcaldy dealer to whom it had sold it for scrap. By the beginning of 1994 virtually all of the physical signs of the Lochty Private Railway had been removed from the site and there is now little to show that there had ever been a railway at this remote corner of Fife.

Back to the Future - the KFRPS

On 21st May, 1992 a company limited by guarantee, the Kingdom of Fife Railway Preservation Society, was formed and as from 1st June of that year was registered as a Scottish charity. The original subscribers to the Memorandum and Articles of Association of the KFRPS were Alastair Douglas, Alex Swanson and Pete Westwater. The object of the Society was to continue with the work of railway preservation in Fife with the specific aim of safekeeping the stock and collections formerly held at Lochty other than No. 16, the observation car and a BSO coach owned by John Cameron himself. The society at that time did not have a permanent site to house its possessions and thus temporary storage was found for its rolling stock at Methil power station thanks to Scottish Power plc and at the yard of Barclay Brothers, haulage contractors, at Methil. The transfer of the stock to its new locations was carried out by a specialist firm, Alleleys, and a film of this event 'Last Train From Lochty' was commissioned by a member of the KFRPS and sold at model railway exhibitions.

The society then looked at various sites to purchase as a permanent home and these included the former Crail Aerodrome, Lochore Meadows, Bowhill Colliery, part of the former Auchtertool branch line, the former Wemyss Private Railway site at Scotts Road in East Wemyss and even the former BR station at Kilconquhar - all of these proved to be unsuitable for various reasons. Then, in 2001, a site was eventually acquired at the east end of the former NBR Kirkland Yard sidings on the outskirts of Leven. A secure compound was then built there and the rolling LPR stock, which had been in temporary storage for almost 10 years, was moved in.

The KFRPS has from then onward continued to restore and preserve its stock and various other artifacts and records and has built a number of sheds and other structures and has laid some track down on which it presently runs its diesel locomotives and stock. The eventual aim is to run steam locomotives in addition to the diesels and to operate a passenger service at Kirkland as part of its ambitious future programme.

Key
- ━━ Existing Network Rail mainline
- ─── Kirkland Yard boundary
- ⋯⋯ Existing compound fence
- ─ ─ Proposed extension of compound fence

- A - Existing Munro Engine Shed
- B - Proposed new storage shed
- C - Platform
- D - Station building
- E - Signal box
- F - Footbridge

KFRPS 2012 plan showing the eventual proposed layout at Kirkland Yard.

Appendix One

A Brief Chronology of the Line

19.10.1892	Meeting in Edinburgh of promoters of line
24.08.1893	East Fife Central Railway Act passed
30.10.1894	Minute of Agreement with NBR signed
06.11.1894	John Howard appointed as contractor
16.07.1895	NBR Act passed involving alterations to line
21.08.1898	Official opening of line
22.08.1898	First public train on EFCR
1898	Baldastard Colliery Siding opened
04.1901	Balcarres Colliery Siding opened
06 1904	Baldastard Colliery Siding closed
12.1906	Balcarres Colliery Siding closed
20.03.1910	Letham Farm Siding opened
12.1911	Largobeath Colliery Siding opened
01.02.1913	Largobeath workmen's trains commence
11.1913	Largobeath workmen's trains withdrawn
01.1916	Largobeath Colliery Siding closed
01.01.1923	London & North Eastern Railway acquire line
01.01.1948	Line nationalized
02.05.1957	Kennoway station unstaffed in summer
06.02.1961	Kennoway, Montrave, Largoward and Lochty permanently unstaffed
10.08.1964	Line closed to all traffic
04.04.1967	No. 9 arrives at Lochty
14.06.1967	Lochty Private Railway opening ceremony
29.03.1970	LPR extended to Knightsward
03.04.1973	No. 9 leaves Lochty for main line
07.04.1973	No. 16 arrives at Lochty
21.05.1992	Kingdom of Fife RPS formed
30.09.1992	LPR closed to traffic.
30.04.1994	Last stock removed from LPR

Note: The opening and closure dates for privately-owned sidings at Baldastard, Balcarres and Largobeath are approximate since no 'official' dates can be traced; the same is also unfortunately the case for Letham Farm Siding.

'J36' No. 65345 on a lightly-loaded Lochty goods at Lathallan, 18th February, 1961.
W.S. Sellar

Appendix Two

Traffic Figures 1900-1934

	Goods (tons)	Minerals (tons)	Coal (tons)	Livestock (head)	Cash remitted (£)
Kennoway					
1900	2,364	168	1,240	1	341
1901	3,157	628	1,208	0	379
1902	3,466	451	1,649	30	434
1903	3,644	355	1,813	0	292
1904	2,893	428	2,177	25	291
1905	3,286	666	2,932	0	230
1906	3,507	343	2,539	13	292
1907	3,053	877	2,596	74	325
1908	2,876	1,106	2,367	8	262
1909	3,826	962	3,288	28	365
1910	2,767	1,181	3,168	19	355
1911	3,246	624	3,235	19	267
1912	5,048	1,471	2,914	2	238
1913	5,231	599	2,592	118	206
1914	4,760	357	2,482	47	274
1915	4,318	311	3,096	36	204
1916	3,410	192	2,566	284	175
1917	7,287	245	2,828	214	131
1918	6,062	383	2,780	117	251
1919	4,549	346	2,770	273	368
1920	4,856	653	2,813	173	640
1921	5,071	490	2,249	130	1,133
1922	3,712	675	2,910	169	689
1923	2,922	722	2,922	685	389
1924	4,596	766	3,084	936	463
1925	4,482	896	2,808	898	312
1926	3,612	1,082	3,080	219	341
1927 (a)	1,156	185	1,729	104	129
Lochty					
1900	680	668	220	292	93
1901	941	223	219	343	83
1902	1,072	223	1,331	218	59
1903	1,050	567	3,010	285	141
1904	672	111	2,855	529	55
1905	1,163	471	1,790	730	51
1906	1,186	314	921	302	51
1907	821	423	415	223	58
1908	687	92	392	144	68
1909	750	292	92	476	52
1910	640	721	59	274	49
1911	687	489	440	79	27
1912	798	514	5,992	128	66
1913	1,089	287	7,547	264	110

APPENDIX

	Goods (tons)	Minerals (tons)	Coal (tons)	Livestock (head)	Cash remitted (£)
Lochty (cont.)					
1914	1,911	1,004	3,472	335	279
1915	1,458	367	753	84	132
1916	2,501	233	853	406	161
1917	1,461	254	758	625	172
1918	1,500	519	866	521	186
1919	1,890	329	848	587	298
1920	2,117	318	790	331	430
1921	1,465	260	528	149	502
1922	1,684	346	605	244	421
1923	1,666	137	613	366	334
1924	1,402	142	549	929	268
1925	1,109	230	502	771	273
1926	939	158	374	849	213
1927	1,073	186	662	1,499	196
1928	870	149	985	479	158
1929	763	98	412	664	121
1930	396	41	456	721	181
1931	419	130	521	486	132
1932	207	26	415	691	106
1933	320	200	384	231	69
1934	284	137	313	388	66
Largoward					
1900	1,692	637	2,990	290	177
1901	2,209	1,141	4,044	96	186
1902	3,008	1,071	2,097	118	236
1903 (*b*)	2,877	414	11,565	207	980
1904 (*b*)	1,990	469	21,972	178	1,675
1905 (*b*)	2,745	514	13,970	56	1,371
1906 (*b*)	3,894	931	8,653	82	895
1907 (*b*)	3,297	1,181	4,929	47	920
1908	3,138	1,131	5,128	111	987
1909	3,455	714	2,523	146	667
1910	2,911	670	1,587	125	393
1911	3,487	5,789	2,866	173	333
1912 (*c*)	3,390	1,136	20,891	73	727
1913 (*c*)	3,541	540	24,880	343	766
1914 (*c*)	2,968	579	7,822	107	143
1915	4,034	435	2,436	358	138
1916	5,517	190	2,385	502	104
1917	4,318	294	2,209	356	149
1918	4,688	109	1,991	110	216
1919	3,266	171	1,816	145	318
1920	5,169	663	1,995	416	660
1921	3,906	42	1,499	559	647
1922	3,324	202	2,085	945	635
1923	3,667	125	1,878	1,253	393
1924	2,853	396	2,049	1,229	498
1925	2,301	407	1,804	1,283	443
1926	2,278	2,063	972	1,138	364

	Goods (tons)	Minerals (tons)	Coal (tons)	Livestock (head)	Cash remitted (£)
Largoward (cont.)					
1927	2,009	408	1,656	2,203	324
1928	1,690	649	1,465	2,192	319
1929	1,479	443	1,324	1,121	199
1930	1,868	3,062	1,342	1,879	191
1931	1,323	749	999	1,287	122
1932	713	206	985	1,314	127
1933	1,194	117	812	1,376	134
1934	1,078	253	798	1,771	108
Montrave					
1900	1,674	2,214	2,951	901	136
1901	2,215	1,904	1,764	511	170
1902	2,791	638	3,443	499	241
1903	2,517	1,275	4,839	723	276
1904	2,719	607	3,649	923	165
1905	3,433	2,689	4,393	899	170
1906	3,086	2,589	3,649	1,280	200
1907	2,823	3,077	4,393	314	167
1908	2,755	2,410	4,669	229	154
1909	2,846	2,025	3,974	343	172
1910	2,022	2,506	3,370	230	115
1911	2,640	3,018	4,291	132	166
1912	3,250	2,415	4,169	111	176
1913	3,583	2,069	3,905	159	222
1914	4,492	1,873	3,275	104	191
1915	5,347	1,172	2,673	326	118
1916	4,811	341	1,942	793	110
1917	6,379	354	1,681	144	115
1918	7,855	530	1,922	29	166
1919	8,700	582	1,724	186	176
1920	7,229	952	1,765	238	222
1921	5,734	404	1,634	187	191
1922	3,465	96	2,129	336	118
1923	3,188	118	2,269	273	359
1924	3,139	472	2,418	689	370
1925	2,584	4,043	2,656	1,371	305
1926	2,839	907	1,199	503	223
1927	2,207	421	1,878	739	209
1928	1,806	1,446	1,585	747	169
1929	1,548	458	1,038	977	148
1930	1,678	1,504	957	560	167
1931	1,400	243	958	945	230
1932	991	97	1,292	997	119
1933	1,904	154	50	578	143
1934	1,208	357	576	180	88

Notes
a – Goods depot closed 1st July 1927 and figures subsumed in Cameron Bridge figures
b – includes Balcarres Colliery Siding
c – Includes Largobeath Colliery Siding

Sources, Acknowledgements and Bibliography

Little has ever appeared in print about the East Fife Central Railway and the authors have, wherever possible, consulted the original documentation held by the National Archives of Scotland in Edinburgh along with the working timetables, notices and other information held in public and private collections and the local newspapers and other paperwork held in Fife libraries and the National Library of Scotland. Much help has been given by a number of individuals who worked or travelled on the line in its LNER or BR days, or on the Lochty Private Railway subsequent to the closure of the branch and the authors would give their thanks to members of the North British Railway Study Group and the Kingdom of Fife Railway Preservation Society. We would recommend that those interested in the history of railways in Fife contact the former at nbrstudygroup.co.uk and to visit the KFRPS on Saturday afternoons at Kirkland Yard or contact them at www.roskotheque.co.kfrps

With apologies for any inadvertent omissions the authors would wish to give their special thanks for the information, photographs and other help given by pre-eminent Fife railway historians Pete Westwater and Alan Brotchie, by John Cameron (who has owned No. 9 for longer than it ever ran on the main line!) and to Alastair Douglas, Donald Cattenach (the historian of George Bradley Wieland), Douglas Hume, Steven Hajducki, George Lees, Alexander Lorimer, Bill Lynn, Donald Mackay, Brian J. Malaws, Bob McGregor, Ed McKenna, Frank Rankin, Douglas Paul, Allan Rodgers, Stuart Sellar, Mike Smith, Hamish Stevenson and David Stirling and also those who are unfortunately no longer with us including the late Ian Addison, John Bennett, Lindsay Horne, Willie Macleod, David Murray, Ed Nicoll, Roger Pedrick and Bill Smith. We are indebted to all of them and would only add that without the help of all of these people this book could not have been written and an interesting chapter of Fife's railway history would have been in danger of being lost for ever. Once again we would also wish to thank Ian Kennedy of our ever patient publishers and one of our greatest supporters and keen promoter of our Fife works, John Barker of East Neuk Books, Anstruther.

Apart from works referred to in the footnotes the following published sources may also be of interest to readers:

Bennett, *Random Reflections of a Roving Railwayman*, (St Andrews, 1975)
Dewar, *Guide and Stocklist to the Lochty Ralway*, (Lochty, 1989)
Forsyth and Chisholm, *the Geology of East Fife* (Edinburgh, 1977)
Hajducki, Jodeluk and Simpson, *The Anstruther & St Andrews Railway* (Usk, 2009) and *The Leven & East of Fife Railway* (Usk, 2013)
Muir, *The Fife Coal Company* (Leven 1952)
Stirling, 'Passengers on the EFC Line', *NBRSG Journal* 54
Rankine (ed), *The East Fife Central Railway* (Leven 1999)
Ransome, *An A4 at Lochty, Steam Alive, 10, 1971.*
RCTS, *Locomotives of the LNER* (various volumes)
Ross, *The North British Railway A History* (Catrine, 2014)
Simpson, 'Further notes on the EFCR', *NBRSG Journal* 73
Smith (ed):*Third Statistical Account of Scotland : The County of Fife* (Edinburgh,1952)
Thomas, *The North British Railway* (2 vols, Newton Abbot, 1968, 1975)
Westwater, *A brief History of the Lochty Private Railway* (Lochty, 1977)
Westwater and Page *Lochty Diary from 1967* and
The First Ten Years - A Short History of the Lochty Private Railway, its Volunteer Staff etc. (Lochty, various dates)

Index

Accidents, 45, 46, 49, 53
Baldastard Colliery, 33, 37, 69
Ballcares Colliery, 35, 37, 69
Bennett, J.M., 45, 46
Briggs, General David, 8, 9, 13, 15, 19, 32
British Railways, 47 *et seq.*
Caledonian Rly, 13
Cameron, John, 83, 84, 87, 96
Cassingray Colliery, 35, 37, 38, 69
Closure, 55, 59, 96
Coal, 8 *et seq.*, 29, 33 *et seq.*, 44, 45
Conacher, John, 15
Cupar, 11, 43, 71
Dobson, David, 41
East Fife Central Railway,
   Capital, 11, 13
   Construction, 16, 17, 19 *et seq.*
   Formation, 13, 15, 16
   Opening, 27, 28
Excursions and workmen's trains, 2, 23, 26, 39, 40, 53 *et seq.*, 78
Gilmour, Sir John, 17, 21, 31, 37, 43
Greenside, 28, 63
Howard, John, 16, 19, 26
Jackson, William, 31
Jordan, John, 9, 13, 15, 31, 32
Kennoway, 16, 23, 28, 39 *et seq.*, 46, 47, 49, 60, 63
Kingdom of Fife RPS, 97 *et seq.*
Knightsward, 69

Landsdale, David, 8, 10, 33
Largobeath Colliery, 38 *et seq.*, 67, 69
Largoward, 7, 8, 21, 25, 35, 37, 38, 45, 57, 59, 65, 66, 71, 73, 74, 79, 81, 101
Largoward Coal Co., 30, 35
Lathallan, 10, 29
Level crossings, 49, 63, 81
Locomotives,
   BR Standard, 51, 77, 80
   Contractors, 20, 22, 25, 26
   Diesel, 81
   Industrial, 35, 89, 96
   North British, 77
Lochty, 10, 11, 14, 15, 21, 23, 26, 27, 45, 47 *et seq.*, 69, 83
Lochty Private Railway, 5, 83 *et seq.*
Meik, Thomas, 15
Montrave, 16, 17, 28, 43, 63, 64, 71
North British Railway, 9, 10, 13, 16, 27 *et seq.*, 33 *et seq.*
Passenger trains, 29 *et seq.*, 87
Planned extensions, 23
Signalling, 38, 39, 61, 81
Snow, 45, 49 *et seq.*
Spot, Major Alexander, 29
Stravithie, 10, 11, 17, 23
Taylor, William, 9, 13, 15
Teasses Lime Co., 15, 37
Wieland, George Bradley, 9, 15, 31, 32

'J36' class 0-6-0 No. 65345 between Kennoway and Montrave, 18th February, 1961.
W.S. Sellar